Project Profitability

Project Profitability

Ensuring Improvement Projects Achieve Maximum Cash ROI

Dr. Reginald Tomas Lee

BEP
BUSINESS EXPERT PRESS
Leader in applied, concise business books

First published in 2022 by
Business Expert Press, LLC
222 East 46th Street, New York, NY 10017
www.businessexpertpress.com

ISBN-13: 978-1-63742-169-7 (paperback)
ISBN-13: 978-1-63742-170-3 (e-book)

Business Expert Press Portfolio and Project Management Collection

Collection ISSN: 2156-8189 (print)
Collection ISSN: 2156-8200 (electronic)

First edition: 2022

10 9 8 7 6 5 4 3 2 1

To Rey
Life is so awesome with you as my son

Description

Consultants and internal project teams often make substantial claims about the savings opportunities resulting from their projects. Oftentimes these claims do not come true. *Project Profitability* explains why these opportunities are not realized and offers a framework that will guarantee your teams identify projects that align with your strategy, calculate cash savings appropriately, and realize these cash savings upon implementation.

Customers of consulting organizations can use this book to keep their consultants honest when savings are promised. Consulting organizations can use this book to help document the value their solutions bring, how much of that value can be realized, and what's necessary to achieve it.

If you are a consultant, you do not want to risk having your customer know the content of this book and challenge the value promise!

Keywords

project ROI; improvement project profitability; project cost–benefit analysis; cash ROI; business domain management; managerial accounting; improving efficiency; capacity management; capacity maps; project implementation; project selection

Contents

Testimonials

"Whether you're a consultant who sells projects or are in charge of project success inside your organization, this book is requisite reading for positioning and assuring a project's worthiness. Dr. Lee helps you understand, articulate, and plan for realizing a project's actual cash value, and illustrates why the oft undefined 'path to savings' within the project plan itself is the crucial element for realizing that value. Turns out there's a distinct difference between 'accounting' value and true cash value which can be misleading or even dangerous to a company's viability. He explains why accounting-department-defined profitability is a detrimental vanity metric and why end cash position is the optimal goal."—**Michelle (Golden) River, CEO, Fore LLC**

"If your position requires you to analyze the ROI or increased efficiencies of projects, then this is a must read. This book could literally save you millions of dollars by analyzing projects based on the cash return instead of perceived savings. 'Perceived' savings might be in a presentation, but not actually realized in the business. Dr. Lee's work in this book has really changed the way I approach the value and savings of projects that I am in charge of."—**Jarrod Souza, CFO at Michael Hyatt and Company**

"Blending an engineer's mind with the historical accounting and finance equation generates clarity to the murky world of business process improvement initiatives. Reginald Lee has expertly prescribed the cure for ineffective business process improvement initiatives by focusing on CROI (cash return on investment). If cash flow is not improved, under what rationale is the business using to invest shareholder value? Project Profitability should be read, underlined, and regularly revisited by any leader responsible for improving the bottom line."—**Daniel D. Morris, CPA, CGMA, TEP; Senior Partner, Morris + D'Angelo, Silicon Valley**

"I have been a fan of Dr. Reginald Tomas Lee for several years. His efforts to reframe the metrics by which organizational projects are evaluated has and continues to challenge the managerial accounting cannon. Project Profitability is his latest addition to a body of work that should be required reading for

every CEO and CFO. Dr. Lee presents clear and compelling evidence that thinking just a little differently about how projects are considered can lead to decisions that increase the likelihood of business success. The subtle, and not so subtle, principles he advances, form a translational space in which established project accounting paradigms are challenged, or even obsoleted, bringing to the fore, decision practices which enable leaders to focus on what matters most—preserving and growing cash. His practical examples, and straight-forward language makes his transformative ideas accessible to all."—**John B. Hammond, Sr. Director, Center for Community Services, Atlanta Regional Commission**

"Dr. Reginald Lee's business domain management framework addresses the glaring cash misses which so often occur on so many company projects. The framework avoids overstating value propositions by focusing on cash and not accounting information, understanding when a project is just right for the company to avoid wasted time on financial justification, and finally ensuring cash is the key objective for project success. This book is a great way to help improve cash generation for any business! Thanks for sharing your insight Dr. Lee!"—**Jeffrey S. Wuest, CEO SynFiny Advisors and Former Finance Executive at P&G**

"Reginald's new book Project Profitability will appeal to both practitioners and academics alike. It is written in a style that is practical and immediately applicable. He provides real world examples that most managers and executives can relate to and challenges leaders to ask tough questions up front to properly scope projects and force realistic estimates of true cash benefits. Having worked directly with Reginald in the past, I know he is a strong advocate for companies to avoid the pitfalls of using traditional accounting methods for project benefit valuation. This book does an excellent job explaining the rationale for taking a different approach to assessing project value and then walks the reader through how to apply it, measure, and track to ensure real cash benefits are realized."—**Greg Soltis, Business Unit President**

"Yet again, Dr. Lee has knocked it out of the park with this book. As a virtual CFO, one of the things my clients struggle with is whether or not to undertake a project and what they should be measuring to make an assessment. Dr. Lee's original thinking on this topic gives a different, much needed, perspective

than what we'd normally consider in the Accounting Domain. I'd highly recommend this book to anybody assessing projects in an organization."—**Chris Hervochon, CPA, CVA, Owner, Chris Hervochon, CPA, CVA LLC**

"In Project Profitability, Dr. Reginald Lee has made another vital contribution to how cost accounting distorts managerial decision making. As a recovering cost accountant, I have to remind myself constantly never to confuse accounting costs, or efficiency gains, or traditional ROI, with cash flow. The focus should be on CROI—Cash ROI. Cash is a measured value. Cost accounting is based on metrics, completely contrived. If you're an accountant, you have some unlearning to do. This book is an excellent guide to learning the correct approach."—**Ronald J. Baker, Radio-Show Host, The Soul of Enterprise: Business in the Knowledge Economy, Founder of VeraSage Institute, and author of the best-selling book, Implementing Value Pricing: A Radical Business Model for Professional Firms, www.thesoulofenterprise.com**

"In the project approval phase, projects can be approved based on a high excitement-factor to capitalize on a new idea for profit or to avoid a threat to the organization. The excitement-factor can be so powerful that it pushes objectivity aside. Later, the lack of objectivity is often revealed as the project falls prey to the realities dismissed during the approval phase and project profitability gives way to rationalization. Reginald Tomas Lee's Project Profitability explores this phenomenon and offers sound guidance to add objectivity into the project approval and execution process that will increase your organization's cash and eliminate the rationalization."—**Jeff Enyart, Former Second Vice President, Finance & FP&A Ohio National Financial Services Really an eye-opening book!**

"This book tells us not only how we can distinguish the difference between cash-flow and accounting but how that difference impacts our profitability in any organization. This isn't just pertinent to engineering projects, but almost all entities such as corporations and NPOs. I'm sure that his new proposal on finance and accounting that is explained in this book could be beneficial to any organization that wants to understand how to make their operations profitable.

I strongly recommend this book to all the managers and engineers in Japanese companies."—竹村和浩 **Takemura Kazuhiro, President and CEO** at Universal Education Inc., Chief Director at SIIC: Smart Inclusion Innovation Consortium. Tokyo, Japan

"As we progress through our careers, I find that reading has become a part of my daily routine. The impact readings are the ones that require a notebook for doodling/scribbling/calculating while you are reading. Reginald has made me evaluate how projects are viewed both financially and culturally. This is going to require a white board and a six pack."—**Joe Morgan, Founder and CEO siY, LLC Former President and Chairman SONY Chemicals Corporation of America Former President and CEO, Board Member Standard Register**

"I highly recommend this book as a thinking tool, which helps you think through real profitability of your projects. As an owner of a small publishing house, I plead guilty: Before meeting Reginald Tomas Lee's work, I didn't understand the difference between cash and non-cash savings. Once upon a time, I decided to decrease printing cost per book, and ordered 3000 copies instead of 1000. Seven years and 2643 books later I am still selling this first print.

As reminder for myself, I will take away this motto from this book: You should watch out for cash return on investment, not only ROI."—**Dmitry Lazarev, OD Consultant, www.lazarev.biz Moscow, Russia**

"As a supply chain professional, I am inundated with requests for multiple initiatives from different functions. However, there is a strong need to evaluate each initiative to ensure that cash value is being realized. This book is a primer to help me in this assessment."—**Matt Anjilivelil, Supply Chain Strategy, Nutrien**

Foreword

"Ed, I pay them anyway."

This five-word reply to what I had considered an artful demonstration of perceived value, halted the processes in my brain. "What?" I muttered.

"Ed, I pay them anyway," my interlocutor repeated.

I had just followed a syllogism that I had traversed hundreds, maybe thousands, of times previously with a prospective customer.

"If I understand correctly, it takes your accounting team, on average, about 23.6 hours to produce your monthly profit and loss statement. Is that right?"

"Yes."

"We have just been able to demonstrate that this time will be cut to an average of 1.8 hours per month, correct?"

"Yes."

"Okay, so if I subtract 1.8 from 23.9 then multiply that by the average wage in the accounting department of $45.67 then multiply that by 12, I estimate we can save you, $12,111.68 per year! How does that sound?"

The five words then shattered what I had thought a magnificent embankment of logic that had led me to victory so often in the past.

I never recovered my composure during that meeting and the deal went down to an ignominious defeat.

It was not until more than a decade later, when reading Dr. Reginald Tomas Lee's earlier book, *Lies, Damn Lies, and Cost Accounting*, that I began to comprehend what had happened and allowed myself to rethink and retool my algorithm to account for what I had missed—I was not "saving" them anything, because the "savings" wasn't CASH!

In this book, *Project Profitability: How to select, justify, and implement projects that achieve maximum cash ROI*, Dr. Lee applies his profound thinking to the internal company project and pleads with us to look beyond the ROI spreadsheet that is ofttimes considered mightier than the sword in far too many organizations.

He challenges us to ignore the legions of cost accountants who think they are the arbiters of profitable decision making by applying their manifold methods as if they were incantations etched in the stone of Mount Sinai.

In true iconoclast fashion, Reginald shatters the stone and slays the mysticism that has been spewed from the mouths of MBAs for the past few decades.

In its place, he crafts for us new bulwark. One impenetrable by the forces of faulty decision making. In short, this book will assist you in making the best possible decisions for you and your organization when considering whether or not to implement a new project in your organization.

—Ed Kless
Senior Fellow, VeraSage Institute
Co-Host, The Soul of Enterprise with Ron Baker
Senior Director, Sage Accountants

Preface

I'd like to propose that companies unknowingly waste and lose billions of dollars annually on improvement projects such as IT solutions, Six-Sigma, lean, process improvement, and equipment-based improvements. It's not to suggest these projects aren't important or valuable, they just do not deliver on the promised savings. Consider the following.

Let's say someone makes the following offer: invest $100 thousand on an improvement project for your organization, and the solution will yield $1 million in savings. The promise may be made by an outside consultant, or even someone who works for your organization—a manager trying to improve her department, for example, or a team of individuals looking to make a difference for the firm. The suggestion is that by eliminating waste, improving quality, or speeding up transactions, the solution makes the workforce 25 percent more efficient. This should, in theory, lead to cost reductions. For each person making $100 thousand that's a $25 thousand savings per person per year. With 40 people in the department, that's $1 million in one year, or $3 million in three years. That's a pretty strong ROI (return on investment), right?

This is how these projects are often justified by those seeking the change and agreed on by those approving the change. We've all seen it and, in many cases, many of us have been responsible for it. I have seen it over and over again, as an engineer, a consultant, and as an academic, where huge value propositions are created to gain project approval, and then the fun begins. The team implements the project, and a very small portion of the savings are realized, sometimes off by an order of magnitude or more. An order of magnitude in the previous case would suggest $100 thousand being the savings versus $1 million. Why does this happen?

There are three primary reasons this happens. First, not all projects are capable of realizing financial returns. Many companies require financial justifications to hire consultants to do work, for example, but a consultant providing a company with a diagnosis of a problem or a way to fix it will not save anything. Creating a financial justification in this case does little good and lots of harm.

Second, the cost–benefit calculations are grossly inadequate. Take the previous example. What does the $25 thousand in savings represent? It's not money, it's a value placed on time. If the 40 people still work for the company at the same salary, not a single penny was saved. Most cost–benefit analyses are accounting based, and accounting costs and benefits such as those described earlier are not money, they're value. Hence, one would have paid $100 thousand to make people more efficient, which is good, but the savings in cash will not occur. Cost–benefit analyses should be cash based. What was spent in cash and what was returned in cash. Most analyses are not as diligent about focusing on cash as they should be if the objective is to make money from the improvement project.

Finally, most companies focus on agreeing to, or actualizing the project. There is less diligence paid to the actual execution of the project for the purposes of realizing cash value. It's the execution where the savings must occur. If the objective is cash savings, oftentimes, the improvement project itself will not create cash savings on its own. Instead, it enables managers to make decisions that will lead to cash savings. It's up to the managers to make and act on the decisions, and for the organization to hold the managers accountable. If managers don't make decisions that affect spending and benefit realization, the benefits will not happen.

I wrote this book to help companies and consultants avoid these issues. The emphasis is on the cash value of projects. As such, accounting costs are dismissed and replaced with a framework that focuses on cash value realization.

For Managers and Executives

This book will focus your teams on the steps and actions required to realize cash value for each of your improvement projects. It will also provide you with information to help you see when consultants and salespeople are trying to pull the wool over your eyes by promising huge savings you will never see.

For Consultants

This book will help you think through your solutions and understand why they generally won't create cash value on its own. Knowing why, you can learn what you can do with your clients to help ensure they take full advantage of the benefits your solutions will enable that will lead to the cash benefits they seek.

Thank you for taking the time to consider these ideas. Some will love them, some will not, but I hope that in some way, you gained some value from these ideas.

Acknowledgments

This book would not have happened without help. First, I'd like to thank God. I have no idea what role He played, but He must have done something because this book is finally finished! There were many times where the words just wouldn't come to me, so I'm gonna go ahead and give that credit to Him. I know some don't buy in, but I do and it's my damn book! Ha-ha.

Second, I'd like to thank Tim Kloppenborg. Tim and I talked about this book a while, back while I was writing *Strategic Cost Transformation*. I thought I'd just be able to knock it out quickly, and I didn't. Tim was very patient and encouraging through the whole process. He was awesome to work with.

Next, I'd like to thank my reviewers, Ed Kless, who also wrote the foreword, and Marianne Novac Davis. It was especially a pleasure having Marianne review my work 15 years after I reviewed her work as her MBA professor. Life is awesome like that. Ed has become a friend, mentor, and intellectual guide. The dude is really cool and wicked smart.

I also want to thank a few folks who have been very strong supporters and encouragers. Glen Johnson was my PhD chair, and it was in that program several decades ago where we came up with the cost/cash management techniques that I still use today. If it weren't for his creativity and willingness to push boundaries, none of this would be possible. Second, I'd like to thank Joe Castellano. Joe, an accounting professor emeritus at the University of Dayton has been a supporter, a reviewer, challenger, and most importantly, a friend. Next, Ron Baker. Ron has been a good friend, an intellectual challenger, and an awesome supporter. Having Ron in my life has been an incredible blessing in so many ways. Finally, I'd like to thank Jeff Enyart. Jeff has been such a strong supporter and reviewer of my work. He always has encouraging things to say and is generous in sharing where and how these ideas can work not only with me but also with the companies with whom he interacts in his career as an extraordinary finance and FP&A leader.

This book would not have been possible without the support of my family. I'll leave the dogs out because I'm convinced they were trying to sabotage the effort with their endless barking at anything and everything. My family supported me and jumped through lots of hoops to allow me to write with relative quiet. My son Reginald Jr, also known as Rey (to whom this book is dedicated) and Tough Man pushed me to finish "his" book. "Is my book finished?" "When are you gonna finish my book?" I had to get it done so I wouldn't disappoint the little guy!

I want to thank a few friends. Rob and Tony of Four80East and Dan and June Kuramoto from Hiroshima for giving me inspiring music as always. This is our 4th or 5th book together with both groups and their inspiring music and creativity. I'd like to thank the staff at Coopers Hawk, my favorite writing place for this book. They kept out of my way and allowed me to work, but made sure I was happy and comfortable. Thanks Amber, Bianca, Jenifer, Nichole, Ray, Shawn, and Shelby. A special thanks to Mark Saadallah, the GM, who would always find a quiet place for me to write when capacity was limited due to Covid and there were no seats to be had. He's also a genuinely good dude.

Finally, as always, I want to thank Pepe, Pedro, Vinny, and Ross for their support through the process.

CHAPTER 1

Lies? Deceit? Deception?

Improvement projects focus on improving the performance of organizations. This includes IT projects, process improvements, lean implementations, and Six-Sigma projects. In most cases, the cash value of these projects is greatly overstated. It is important to understand *that* this happens and *why* it happens so that we can avoid investing in projects that will not pay off from a cash perspective.

A friend works for a software company that focuses on budgeting. One day, we were having a conversation where we compared notes regarding how his company's software handles cash versus how my Business Domain Management or BDM model handles cash. During the conversation, he mentioned that one of his clients, a very large well-known company, was going to reduce costs by $1 billion. One. Billion. Dollars. Sounds pretty impressive! I asked him if he was sure about that number and his response was an enthusiastic, "Yes!"

Let's think about this. What would it take to save $1 billion? If we tried to save it in one year using staff reductions alone, that would involve getting rid of 10 thousand people each making $100 thousand per year. Even that wouldn't cover it, since there would likely be a severance package, which would mean the total salary would not be saved. A quick check showed the company had 135 thousand people working for it in 2020. The company has many retail locations suggesting that most of the 135 thousand would not be making $100 thousand. Another alternative would be to get rid of 20 thousand people making $50 thousand per year. That would allow for a much wider net to be cast, of course, but that's still a significant number of people. Will this company have the appetite to make such cuts, or is it all hype?

When it comes to value and saving money, there are a substantial number of lies, cases of deceit, and acts of deception to wade through to find true answers. Consider the following three scenarios.

Scenario 1

A customer of mine was approached by another consulting firm operating as a software vendor. The vendor promised $20 million in savings from their solution. My client sold large technology infrastructures that their customers, in turn, used to provide services to their clients. The vendor offered what is called a configurator as their solution. The configurator would allow my customer's clients to design, or configure, their own infrastructure rather than have my customer's engineers do the configuration for them. The vendor's argument was, if the customers do the configuring instead of our clients' engineers, the savings opportunity would be $20 million. My client asked if this were true.

The first thing we wondered was, "Would the customers even use the configurator?" So, we asked them. None of their largest customers would use it. Their customers felt they needed the expertise of the engineers to manage risks and factors their own engineers may not be in the position to understand. For this to be successful, the customers would have to cooperate. If the vendor is promising $20 million in savings, for a 4:1 cash ROI, the company would sell their solution for $4 million. If true, my client was paying $4 million, let's say, for a solution that wasn't going to be used by their customers. Next, we asked the client whether they were willing to part with $20 million worth of engineers. That would be 200 engineers at $100 thousand each. The answer was a resounding "No." With no one willing to use the software and with the company choosing to avoid labor reductions, one must question the real cash value of the solution.

The software vendor, and their overstated value, had been exposed.

Scenario 2

The next scenario involved a company I worked for. I was asked to come in and validate a $50M value proposition to support a substantial software implementation and the associated consulting work. The software implementation and consulting were going to cost north of $20 million. After analyzing their numbers, $50 million was not only wrong, it was off by an order of magnitude! $5 million would have been extraordinarily generous. To achieve $50 million in cash, the company would have to reduce spend by $50 million. When the company was asked about whether they had the appetite to reduce their workforce by 500 people making $100K per year, again, the answer was, "No." Hence, another hyper value-opportunity was identified before a potentially disastrous situation involving investing a significant amount of money without the desired savings being realized or realizable.

Scenario 3

This scenario involved another software vendor attempting to sell their software to another customer of mine.

Vendor: If you buy our warehouse management software, you will save $4 million.
Customer: How?
Vendor: Faster information, increased productivity …
Customer: I agree that's true. How am I going to save $4 million?
Vendor: Better quality data, improved decision making …
Customer: I agree with all that. I need to know how your solution is going to enable me to spend *four million fewer dollars*.
Vendor: Put that way, I can't.
Customer: Ok. I'll take the software. I believe your solution has value, but I don't want to be on the hook for providing $4 million in cash savings that I know isn't there.

Imagine you're the executive who pulled the trigger on any one of these scenarios, where there was a significant promise of value that, without looking into it, was not possible. How would it affect your company? Your job or career?

What's common among all of these scenarios? First, the vendors, including my employer, each offered substantial value propositions; numbers that would more than cover the price of an expensive software purchase and the associated consulting. Second, the calculation of the value proposition was incorrect in each case if the objectives were to generate cash savings to offset the cash investment in the solution. An example of the technique used to calculate such value propositions is this; the average person in this position makes $100 thousand per year. If we make them 10 percent more efficient with our solution, we will save $10 thousand. With 20 of them working here, we will save $200 thousand. This may be considered a pretty robust value proposition. However, if the now more efficient people are still working there, you've not spent $200 thousand less.

Improvement Projects

Each scenario was a potential improvement project. Improvement projects are designed to improve the performance of companies in multiple ways: improving financially, operationally, or improving or fixing compliance-related issues. In most cases, the objective is to have the improvement projects generate more in savings than it cost the company to realize the savings. If we were going to spend $1 million on an improvement project, we generally want the benefit to be well north of $1 million.

Although notionally correct, it's not always practical. Sometimes there is no financial value that can be placed on a project. Take compliance. What dollar value do you put on a project that helps an executive avoid prison, for example? Of course, one can calculate fines that were avoided by the company, but if your company is delisted from the stock exchange, how do you put a number on that? Second, sometimes business processes just need to be improved. Newer technology, faster and better quality information, and updating to new industry standards can all be good things whether there is a cash value proposition tied to it or not. Sometimes, one must bite the bullet, invest, and realize the value the project delivers, whether it's financial or not. Additionally, not all projects should be forced to require a cash return. Improvement projects are often generally good for the company. Requiring a financial return can sometimes lead to the creation of bogus value propositions. If an improvement opportunity is going to cost $1 million, we'd better find $6 million for a 5:1 ROI if that's our company's stated requirement. So, what do people do? They try to capture each and every source of value they can find, whether it is legitimate or not.

One department at a university wanted to create a maintenance depot for the vehicles it was responsible for. The department managed many, but not all the university's vehicles. Considering only the vehicles that fell under the director's purview, the savings opportunities were not large enough. So, what did she do? She decided to include every area that is remotely tied to, or related to hers, and that also needed vehicles serviced. She expanded the scope of what her opportunity could reasonably cover by including areas where she had discussed her solution with those responsible for vehicles other than hers. Discussing, however, does not mean they had committed to using, or even supporting her solution.

The latter is a dangerous and highly questionable business practice. It is dangerous because of benefit value inflation and, as a result, value is overpromised.[1] This can lead to investments in improvement opportunities that may otherwise be avoided. When leaders make decisions that involve committing significant resources, especially financial resources, they should be privy to the true value opportunity their investment should create or enable. This means there should be clear definitions or descriptions of the operational-, financial-, and compliance-based value that can result from the project. If the true cash savings is $50 million, great! If, instead, the true value is less than $5 million, leaders should know this because it might impact the decision calculus substantially. This will allow them to make decisions based on sound, objective data, and information. Creating fictitious value where it doesn't exist may cause companies to invest in projects that will not create the returns promised or, potentially worse, cause leaders to invest in these projects rather than projects that are more strategically important or more financially viable and desirable. Imagine working in a cash-strapped company and leadership chose and spent $1 million on a project that promised $2 million

---

[1] R.T. Lee. November/December, 2015. How we overstate ROI on improvement projects. *Cost Management*, pp. 16–20.

and delivered a total of $500 thousand cash for a loss of $500 thousand in cash versus your project, which would have required the company to spend $200 thousand on a project that both promised and would generate $300 thousand in cash.

This book was written to address these issues. Primarily, how do we determine whether an improvement project will, in fact, be cash-wise profitable? We will see that there are two types of profit: accounting profit and cash profit. There is a difference, and this difference is significant as we will see throughout this book. The only focus of this book is on generating cash profit. With cash profit, we're talking about making money, not as defined on accounting statements and by managerial accountants, but instead, by looking at the only way a company's cash can be affected; the rates cash enters and leaves the organization.

We will see that it is the loose application of accounting-based techniques and assumptions that lead to the lies, deceit, and deception. The lies, deceit, and deception are tied to the false promises of value, which often stem from how we look at, interpret, and use accounting information. We will understand how the deceit occurs and how to keep it from happening in our organizations. This, in turn, will eliminate the creation of impossibly large value propositions and will create ammunition for those in your firm to see through the substantial, but artificial value propositions offered by consultants and others trying to sell products and services to your firm. This will result in investments that are more tactically and strategically valuable to your firm.

In addition to this there are two other key issues that the book will cover. First, is the importance of project prioritization in the contexts of project type and the strategic importance, or salience, of the process being considered for improvement. Some projects cannot deliver financial benefits based on the project type and what the project is designed to deliver. Additionally, some processes stand out, or are more strategically salient than others. We will want to understand how to identify processes that are more strategically salient to ensure they are strongly considered for improvement, especially when there is limited time and money. This combination will give us a prioritization schema that considers the combination of process salience and the type of project, which will be discussed in detail in Chapter 5.

The second, which is the area we will focus on overall, will be the implementation phase of improvement projects. For many companies, the effort is placed on defining the project and the cost–benefit analysis, or CBA. However, the implementation is where the rubber meets the road. We will find that, in most cases, implementing the project is only the beginning of the cash value realization process. To receive financial value, often, there will need to be management action—steps that will change the organization in a way that will help the company realize the cash benefits from the improvement. Go back to the configurator example. Management action would involve actually cutting engineers to achieve the $20 million. For the $50 million project customer to have to get rid of people and facilities, for them to realize the $50 million saving. Software solutions, themselves, will not sell your facilities or lay off your team.

In order, we will begin by discussing the process of selecting, validating, and implementing projects. We will then dive deeply into these areas and demonstrate how, when these three work together, companies can ensure their improvement projects will generate cash for the organization. Before that, however, we will spend time focusing on cash by creating a baseline understanding of cash and what affects it. The next chapter will help us think through the idea of what it takes to create cash value through the use of improvement projects.

Key Takeaways

1. Many projects will overstate their value propositions. This is due to relying on and using accounting information to describe the value.
2. Not all projects should be forced to have a financial justification. Sometimes they're just good for the company. We will want to understand the financial implications, of course, but that should not always require a positive payback to move forward.
3. Realizing cash value, not accounting profit value, should be the key objective for those projects that can, and should, realize a positive financial return. Cash value realization will, in most cases, require management action for cash returns to be realized.

CHAPTER 2

The Cash Value Realization Process

Cash value realization does not just happen. It takes diligence and an effective process that leads your firm down the path to cash value realization. This involves selecting the right projects, justifying them from a cash perspective while distinguishing the differences between cash and noncash costs and improvements, planning the implementation, and executing the implementation plan with an emphasis on value realization.

Lean. Six-Sigma. IT investments. Business transformations. There are several ways companies look to increase business performance. Key elements to this increase in performance are the improvement projects that companies undertake. Although these improvements may include both operational and financial performance, there is a general expectation that the project will make money for the organization. That doesn't mean they always do or need to. There may be situations such as safety or compliance issues that a project must address and the solution may not be the type that will lead to financial improvements.

The money we expect improvement projects to make should both cover the cash cost of the project and generate more money than it would have, had the project not been implemented. In other words, it is expected that the project will be cash-wise profitable. However, many that intend to be are not, and even more do not live up to the promises made in terms of the value that the project delivered.

Consider the software company, Oracle. Several years ago, they announced their company would save $500 million using their own software tools as a basis for the improvement. This number was later increased to $2 billion.[1] Reviews of their financials suggested the savings were not there, either from an accounting perspective or a cash perspective.[2] Think, for a moment, about what it would take for a company to save $2 billion in cash. Using a quick "back of the napkin" approach similar to the company mentioned at the beginning of Chapter 1, it would be the equivalent of laying off 20,000 people making $100K per year. There was nothing even remotely close to that on their books or in the press. Such a change is significant. If the company known for their ERP software and consulting capabilities is misrepresenting the value their own solutions create internally, how can we expect them to represent value any better for others?

Consider the billions of dollars spent on large global consultancies such as the Big 4, McKinsey, Tata, Infosys, and all the others. There is an expectation they will improve financial performance by reducing costs and improving profit. Let's say the global spend on all consultancies is an even $200 billion. To get a 5:1 cash ROI, they would need to find $1.2 trillion in cash and not accounting cost reductions, which aren't really cash.[3] I mean real money.[4]

There is no evidence that $1.2 trillion is being created annually by these consultancies and the improvement projects they're selling to their customers. There should be evidence—a smoking gun, because $1.2 trillion is a significant amount of money. These consultancies most likely created business cases for their work, and these business cases likely suggested their customers would realize the $1.2 trillion in aggregate. Why would their customers buy projects that cost tens of millions of dollars if there weren't justification for the investment? They generally wouldn't, so we should be able to find the value.

What about the consultants themselves and their own descriptions of their cost-cutting exploits? Throughout my career in the cash

---

[1] S. Leibs. July 01, 2000. "ORACLE'S billion-dollar BOAST." Retrieved March 05, 2020, from www.cfo.com/2000/07/oracles-billion-dollar-boast/

[2] R.T. Yu-Lee. July-August, 2005. "Margin Improvement: More than a notion?" *Industrial Management,* pp. 21–26.

[3] R.T. Lee. 2018. "Strategic Cost Transformation: Using Business Domain Management to Improve Cost Data, Analysis, and Management." *Business Expert Press.*

[4] I will show that accounting cost reduction is not real cash.

improvement space, I've heard countless consultants brag about how much "money" they've saved companies or how focused their solutions are on cost savings. They wear their *results* as a badge of honor; "I, alone, have saved companies a total of a billion dollars over my career!" Considering the executive's question in Scenario 3 in Chapter 1, where is the proof that companies spent $1 billion less in cash with this consultant, or $1.2 trillion less in cash annually with the various consultancies? In most cases, a little due diligence will show that the promised dollar savings are simply not there in cash.

The problem is not that consultants and consultancies are intentionally lying and offering false promises. They just don't know any better. They believe what their approaches are telling them. However, the processes and techniques they use are ineffective when it comes to understanding and calculating cost savings from a cash perspective. Additionally, the approaches are based on outdated and mathematically inaccurate accounting-based models. What makes the situation worse is the notion that the consultants' prospects do not have effective processes to both challenge the consultants' promises of significant savings and to take the project from concept to value realization via their own improvement project process or methodology.

An effective approach to addressing both concerns would include effective cash-based value quantification and an implementation process that would limit the influence and impact of the lies and false promises would have on decision making. Let's look at this in more detail.

The Process to Achieve Value

A process is a step or series of steps that convert some beginning points or inputs into an ending point, outcome, or set of outcomes. For instance, there are processes involved with hiring someone, paying invoices, repairing a customer's furnace, or creating a product that will be sold to the market. Value realization processes should start with an input, which could be a problem or ideas of where the company should improve, such as underperforming processes or people, high costs, low output rates, or poor quality, and then performing the steps of the process, leading to the creation of a tangible, cash-based outcome for the purposes of this book.

In general, when it comes to process performance, not all processes are the same. Some processes use available inputs or capacity such as people, technology, materials, and space, to create output better, more efficiently or more effectively than others. Some are faster or produce fewer errors than others. Some create more goodwill with the market than others.

When looking at processes and process performance, one can create a scale that represents process performance and effectiveness. This scale can be used to assess key performance attributes of a process. An example of a scale is shown in Figure 2.1. They generally go from a process not existing at all (0), as is the case with ad hoc processes in start-up companies, for instance, to well-defined, best-in-class processes you may find with highly functioning, well established organizations (4).

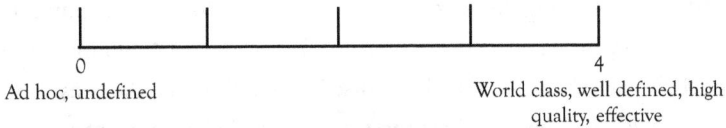

0   4
Ad hoc, undefined   World class, well defined, high
                                                    quality, effective

Figure 2.1 Processes can be assessed by looking at and plotting their capabilities on a defined scale. When doing so, it's important to avoid the likely politics that will surface by having a third party, whether internal or external, review the work. Fewer people than there should be will agree to the idea that the process they oversee is underperforming

In this example and in my own work, I use 0 to 4, but the scale can be changed to whatever fits your purpose. However, it needs to be functional and provide enough clarity in terms of creating performance differentiation at each point on the scale. For instance, with just two points, the options are pretty limited. This may create a binary situation where either the process does something, or it doesn't. With too many steps, the arguments end up being one of differentiation; "Why is this a 7 and not an 8?" If there are not clear and concise definitions between the two, arguments may ensue about a particular rank or value chosen, which can hamper progress.

The suggestion here is to assess both the value realization process and related subprocesses using this scale to determine how effective and mature the processes are and to find any deficiencies in the processes that can be improved to deliver greater value. It should be noted that the assessment should be performed by as neutral of a party as possible to avoid any biases regarding how effectively the process is performing.

To understand how this works, think about accounts payable at a start-up firm. Several people at the firm buy products individually that they use for work and either pay themselves or they are sent an invoice. If not paid for when the transaction takes place, they may pay the invoice at a later date themselves and request reimbursements from Susan, also known as the accounting department, in an e-mail or in a passing conversation. Sometimes they may submit the invoice to Susan and ask her to pay it directly. Susan may also combine it with other invoices from the same vendor and pay all that are due when she has time or during her designated accounts payable periods.

That is the level of sophistication that this process has within the organization. We see there is no formal process to pay the vendor. They just do what makes sense or is convenient at that moment. There may not be any matching of the invoice to what was purchased or received. There may be no consideration regarding available pricing discounts per a contract or review of the accuracy of pricing. There may be no consideration for the timing of the payment and possible discounts available for early payment and when no discounts are available, consideration for the best time to pay the invoice to improve working capital management. There are no checks to see whether there are penalties for late payments or whether the bill had already been paid by someone else. Instead, she just sends a check based on a request for her to do so. Invoices arrive and someone hopefully pays them. This would be considered more of an ad hoc process; no standardization, rules, repeatability, metrics, controls, or governance.

On the other end of the scale, there is a well-thought-out formal process that is automated, documented, repeatable, effective, efficient, fast, with proper controls, and low risk. Purchases are made via the company's e-procurement system. All invoices are sent electronically to a processing center, which could still be Susan, where the data on the invoice are automatically checked against a contract and against the actual transaction: what was bought, received, when, and by whom? The system automatically verifies that the invoice has not been paid previously to eliminate duplicate payments. It then checks to find the ideal time to pay the invoices to optimize working capital. If there is a reduction in price for early payments, the payment will be sent electronically at a time that will follow the terms to realize the reduction, but not sooner. If there is no discount, payment will be made on the due date and not before, so the company can hold on to its cash for investment purposes. A process like this may be on the opposite end of the scale.

Reconsidering value realization, most companies have processes with capabilities that are somewhere in the middle of this scale. Based on my experience, if I were to plot the value realization processes that I've seen in organizations large and small, most would tend to be on the left side of the scale; many on the far left. The process may not be defined, documented, or repeatable with standard procedures, techniques, or controls in place. In other instances, these factors may be in place, but they are often rudimentary.

Consider the process of justifying improvement projects financially. At a high level, we know we need the project scope, objectives, plan, tasks, and deliverables, a CBA, and an approval from management, so we prepare them all for review and consideration. Each iteration looks different and uses different techniques and assumptions to determine scope, assess strategic importance to the company, and to calculate, and analyze the benefits. There is no standard way to categorize and prioritize potential projects.

With such approaches come risks. How does one know the approach used appropriately represents the value opportunity? Did they use acceptable tools, techniques, and assumptions to represent the projects? How does one compare projects, investment opportunities, and returns if each team uses a bespoke approach? How do we know one investment opportunity is better than another in terms of the importance of the process in the eyes of customers or its ability to create cash returns for the firm?

Companies with more evolved processes will generally focus on standardization, efficiency, and effectiveness. There may be, for example, one technique or template for CBAs, and a formal review of project opportunities. However, a full blown, highly effective process for selecting, justifying, and realizing the value may still not exist. Even if it did that would still not guarantee success. Let's think about why.

Ineffective Steps to Cash Value

When one looks at a cash value realization process, oftentimes the steps are ineffective in the context of how they guide companies along the path to value. There are generally five steps along the path to cash value realization:

1. Project identification and selection;
2. Project justification;
3. Define path to value realization;
4. Benefit articulation and projection;
5. Implementation and value realization.

Let's consider in turn.

Project Identification and Selection

The first step in identifying improvement opportunities is asking whether there is truly a problem or opportunity. In their book, *Let's Get Real or Let's Not Play*, the authors, Mayan Khalsa and Randy Illig make a strong argument for justifying whether there is truly a problem deserving of improvement or change and understanding more about why it may or may not be a problem. We may believe there is a problem notionally, but what proof is there? How do we know there is a problem? To address these issues, the authors offer an "opportunity checklist" that companies should consider when looking at improvement opportunities:

Issues: What problems or results [are we] trying to address? In what priority?

Evidence: How do we define the problem? How do we measure success?

Impact: What are the financial, [nonfinancial], and intangible costs and benefits?

Context: Who or what else is affected by the issues and the solution?

Constraints: What has stopped (or might stop) the organization from resolving these issues?[5]

---

[5] M. Khalsa and R. Illig. 2008. *Let's Get Real or Let's Not Play: Transforming the Buyer/Seller Relationship*, 72. New York: Portfolio.

I find this to be a very good way to start down the process of identifying improvement opportunities. From personal experience, many individuals in organizations don't have an effective approach to ensure there is, in fact, a problem worthy of being addressed. They talk past each other, create assumptions about issues without gathering facts, use terms without an agreed upon operating definition, and assume we are talking about, and addressing the same problem without having defined the problem effectively.

The evidence portion is critical, yet oftentimes, we don't pay enough attention to it. How do we know we have a problem? When we fix it, how do we know we're successful? In some cases, it's clear and in others, it's nonexistent. For instance, I was asked to serve on a diversity and inclusion initiative committee at a university. In the first meeting, there was talk about creating a mentorship program for minority faculty. I asked if we knew there was a problem and although many answered in the affirmative, no one had any actual proof. There were no data presented that supported this notion and the problem the mentorship program was supposed to address had not been defined. Hence, the group was looking to create a solution to a problem that had not been defined or proven to be an issue.

How do you create a solution to address something that has not been defined? How would success be determined? We could have spent money to address a problem that may not even exist, and true success would be fleeting if it existed at all because there was no problem resolution defined for the solution to address. Without asking tough questions such as those proposed by Khalsa and Illig, companies can needlessly chase opportunities, wasting money and other resources along the way.

With impact, we want to create an understanding of what success will be to the organization. Will there be improvements in profit? Cash? Will we free up capacity for other uses? Are the improvements difficult to measure, but nevertheless important, such as when we consider factors like goodwill? Context, too, is important here. Whose work or output is affected by the issue, and how will they be affected by the solution, both positively and negatively?

Lastly, if this is an issue or problem for the organization, what has kept the organization from fixing it in the past? Will the previous resistance or lack of action create constraints in moving forward? One may define a solution that seems grand or obvious. Key questions may be, "If this is such a great idea, why haven't we implemented it before?" or "Have we tried this before, and if so, why wasn't it successful?" Such questions identify potential red flags that may obstruct the value realization process.

Thinking through these factors will help validate whether the problem is something worth considering at all.

The second step in project identification and selection is considering the extent to which the improvement opportunity is aligned with the corporate strategy. It's likely that at any given point in time for a larger organization, multiple people will find problems related to their areas. In fact, there is often no shortage of improvement project opportunities for companies of all sizes. The question is, which projects should they select, and which are either shelved or thrown out altogether? The justification is often value based, anecdotal, or politically motivated. What you don't often see are the following two scenarios.

Scenario 1

Alignment with the corporate strategy should be an important criterion when considering improvement projects. This will ensure improvement efforts and the requisite investments in them will have an impact on the execution of the strategy. The process of considering and ensuring strategic alignment forces us to consider the strategic importance of the project, and as a result, should play an important role in the prioritization process.

When strategic alignment isn't considered, decisions can be made that may not be effective in advancing the strategy. Let's say process A is customer facing and is important to sales and growth. Process B is a back-office process that touches many people and has a highly vocal leader speaking in support of the improvement opportunity. If they have the same savings potential, there are limited funds for investment, and failing to fix process B will not lead to general outrage by employees, which one should you choose? It's quite possible the back-office project may be selected, even though the customer facing process may be more strategically important because it is market facing.

This happens quite frequently. Why? Oftentimes, the issue being addressed may resonate more because the process is internal, may be seen by, or affect more people, and the negative effects of the poor process may appear to be greater than the one that is outward facing. This may cause the issue to be fresher or more salient in the minds of those involved in making the decision. It doesn't hurt that the need for the improvement is made by a more outspoken leader. As a result, it may appear that this project should have a higher priority than the customer facing project.

Without an approach that sets clear parameters for strategic alignment, the selection process may be about fire and thunder, politics, emotion, or persuasion rather than the facts of the situation and what is truly most important for the company's future growth and brand. Sometimes it's better to invest in the back-office opportunity. However, in many cases, it's more important to invest in those processes that affect relationships with the customer, sales, and market growth. We need, then, a set of criteria that will help us understand these circumstances and guide us toward this decision rather than relying on an ad hoc, discussion-based, anecdotal and politically driven decision-making process.

Having a process to assess strategic alignment is not about excluding processes because they're deemed less important. Although certain processes and functional areas may have greater alignment with the strategy than others, this says nothing about relative importance of the process. All areas are important and play a role in the functioning of the organization. However, for a product-based company, product development may be more aligned with the corporate strategy than, for example, accounts payable. The improvement project selection process should recognize and acknowledge this and take a process's strategic alignment into consideration when prioritizing projects.

Scenario 2

The next factor that is often overlooked is the type of project being proposed. There are generally three types of projects that companies buy or execute: information, plan, or implementation. The project type influences the cash savings potential and the timing. This will create context for what to expect in terms of benefit realization opportunities and when you can expect the benefits to occur. It will also provide context for what circumstances will lead to cash benefits and which will not. We know, for instance, that cash benefits will come primarily from implementing or executing a project. If you do not implement, you will not see cash improvements.

Going back to Chapter 1, companies may require a financial justification for every major expenditure, whether there is cash value or not. When there is no justification and you need it, what do you do? You make it up. To illustrate, let's say you have a division of a company you're looking to sell, and you engage a consulting firm for help. There may be elements of the opportunity for which you need clarity, so you hire the consultants to help you figure them out. The information they provide may be of value to you, but the result of their work, alone, will not lead to direct cash improvements for the organization. Hence, there will be no direct cash ROI.

However, I've seen financial justifications for projects that will only provide information, such as strategy projects and risk assessments. Information itself has no cash value proposition. It's only when you act on information that cash can be affected. However, there may be a value proposition requirement imposed by leadership; "If we hire these consultants, what will be the benefit? We need a financial justification for this $1M." In reality, these projects themselves save absolutely nothing. The savings are tied to the execution. So, what do you do? Do you start guessing at what the post implementation value of their benefit would be without even knowing what they will find and propose? How effective of a management approach is that? This isn't to suggest information projects are not important. The information may be very important and highly valuable. However, requiring teams to document financial value for a project that cannot deliver it makes little managerial sense.

With project selection, there needs to be contextual information that will help prioritize projects based on project type when resources, budget, or time are limited.

The combination of the strategic importance to the company and the type of projects the company is considering can help leaders focus the company on which improvement project they should invest their cash, all things being equal. We will discuss this in more detail in Chapter 5.

Project Justification

The CBA, has several names, but the concept remains the same; what will the project cost and what financial benefits will be realized as a result of its implementation? For the purposes of this book and the cash value realization process, all CBAs should be cash focused. This does not mean other elements should not be considered. On the contrary, throughout the book, I will discuss noncash benefits and how to model them using capacity maps, but the main purpose of this book is specifically creating cash value.

There are typically four problems companies run into when attempting to create a cash-based a CBA:

1. Project costs aren't always cash;
2. The benefits do not distinguish cash cost savings from noncash cost savings;
3. The size of the financial benefit is often inflated;
4. Lack of clarity regarding how to achieve the real cash savings opportunities.

Let's discuss each briefly now, and in more detail later in the book.

Project Costs Aren't Always Cash

The cost portion of the CBA typically focuses on the cost of the project and any associated fees. The key questions to be considered are, "What is the cost?" and a second, often overlooked question is, "Cost *to whom?*"

Consider labor costs for an IT project. A company has an internal resource who charges a department budget $60 per hour for her IT-related work. Compare this to having an external resource who charges $60 per hour to the same project budget. The manager overseeing the budget and asking the question "What is the cost?" will see the $60 per hour is the same with either resource. When she asks "Cost to whom?" there is a different story.

To her company, there is a significant difference. The $60 per hour internal employee works at the firm and is often salaried. This means she will be paid whether she works on the project or not. Her firm has committed to paying her to do her job, which may or may not include the project for which she is being considered. Her salary is the money spent by the company and has nothing to do, abstractly, with the work she is doing.[6]

---

[6] Lee 2018.

The external resource causes the firm to spend additional money; money that would not have been spent otherwise. In other words, when they hire the additional resource, an additional $60 leaves the company for every hour of work, which, again, is *not* the case for the internal worker. In a worst case scenario, if the internal IT resource works for the company yet the project manager chooses the outside resource instead citing the same cost, the company is actually in a worse situation. The money paid outside the firm means the firm pays for the IT staff employee *and* for the external support, which is a greater cash hit to the firm.

There is a cash cost associated with hiring the outside resource. An example of a cash cost is something for which there is a cash transaction.[7] For instance, when you buy materials for inventory, there will be a cash transaction associated with paying for the inventory. However, when you consume the material you bought, there is no cash transaction involved.[8] You can put a value on the material consumed just as you could for an hour of the inside IT staffer's time but imputing a cost does not automatically make the resulting financial value monetarily based.

An example I like to use as to illustrate this point is the following. Assume I like to bake, and I bought a 10-pound bag of flour for $10. The cash transaction was $10 for 10 pounds of flour. If I use one pound of the flour, I can say the *cost* of the flour used is one dollar. However, there was no cash transaction for one dollar when I use the flour I had already paid for. And the one dollar isn't exact either. If I use one pound and throw away the remaining nine pounds, is that one pound still worth $1 or is it worth $10? The answer is "it depends." We will see later in the book the $1 is a function of how we chose to calculate the cost. It could just as easily have been 79¢ or $1.24. If it were a cash cost, however, it would not depend on any extraneous factors. Cash is exact; its value and quantity are solid and irrefutable. That we paid $10 for the flour or not is indisputable; what is disputable is how we choose to value the one pound of flour we consumed.

---

[7] R.T. Lee. 2016. "Lies, Damned Lies, and Cost Accounting: How Capacity Management Enables Improved Cost and Cash Flow Management," *Business Expert Press*.

[8] Ibid.

This will be important when considering value quantification. Some attempt to dismiss this notion of noncash and cash costs as the difference between soft and hard costs, and suggest hard costs are cash oriented. Few things could be further from the truth. There are some seemingly very hard costs that, when reduced, have no cash savings at all. In fact, they have nothing to do with cash. Consider one of the hardest costs there is, product costs. Product costs are composed of direct material, direct labor, and overhead costs. Direct materials and labor are considered variable costs in accounting because their values "change" with output. Because they are "clear" and documentable, we focus on them and trying to reduce them so we can improve our margins, our profitability.

Going back to the baking example where the $1 for flour can be practically any value between $0 and $10 as a direct material cost, companies often look at these costs and consider them hard costs. However, we will see both in the next section and the next chapter, these costs are as soft, mathematically, as something like the "cost" of goodwill and will have nothing to do with cash. Hard and soft costs are defined in the context of accounting information but not in the context of cash transactions.

Benefits Do Not Distinguish Cash and Noncash Costs

As with the costs of the project, there are cash and noncash benefits as well. Going back to the flour example, let's say we have a laborer we pay $20 per hour. Assume she can make five loaves of bread per hour. We choose to divide her $20 by output to calculate a labor cost of $4 per loaf while maintaining the $1 per pound material cost. Assume a new technique or technology comes all that allows her to miraculously increase her output from 5 to 10 per hour. This is assumed to reduce the cost to produce the unit from $5 ($4 labor and $1 materials) to $3 ($2 labor and $1 materials). We still pay $10 for every 10-pound bag of flour and $20 for each hour of labor. Nothing has changed from a cash perspective. However, if we take advantage of the improvement and make loaves faster, our output rate will increase. If so, since we are going through the flour at a faster rate, cash leaving the company will increases because we are buying more materials. So, where is $2 being saved from a cash perspective? The answer is, there isn't $2 cash being saved.

This is a noncash improvement. Just considering the cash of the matter, we paid for the 10 pounds of flour to be there. It is available to be used whether we use it or not. Additionally, the cash we paid to have this flour will not change as a result of consuming it. The same happens with labor. What we paid the worker did not change with output. If she is there on the clock, she will get her $20 whether she produces 5, 10, 0, or an infinite number of loaves. The cash, in this situation, does not change even though there is a calculated cost savings to what is typically considered a hard cost.[9]

Noncash costs result from calculated accounting costs. If you must figure out what something costs, chances are, it's not a cash cost.[10] For instance, we knew we paid the laborer $20 to work one hour. That is clear. However, when you want a labor cost for a loaf, you must figure it out. Do you take the total output created and divide that into the hourly pay rate as I did? Do you come up with a cost per minute rate? For instance, for the laborer making five units per hour, the cost per unit may be $4 using the previous calculation of dividing the hourly wage by output. However, what if each loaf takes nine minutes to make? Now, we're consuming 45 minutes rather than the full 60 minutes. If we have a calculated cost of 33¢ per minute ($20÷60 minutes), that suggests each loaf costs $3 in labor, not $4. In either case, the cash remains the same. What is different is how you put a value on the consumption of the labor.

As we will see throughout this book, it will be very important to understand the difference between cash and noncash savings. You may be asking yourself, "What does this have to do with improvement projects?" Well, a lot. This is how value propositions are often calculated. I've often heard consultants and software salespeople say they can make your $2 million department 5 percent more efficient, saving you $50K. This is

---

[9] Some may suggest, "Yes, but we can sell more." There are three issues with this statement. First, sales is a revenue issue, not a cost issue. Second, there is an assumption that there is demand for the increased output. This may not be the case. Third, not all processes create salable output, so this suggestion is not generally applicable to improvements throughout the organization.

[10] Ibid.

how the $20 million and $50 million software value propositions mentioned in Chapter 1 were calculated.

This technique leads to totally bogus values placed on improvements. Let's go back to Oracle. According to CFO magazine, "only a small portion (about 13 percent) of the $2 billion gain Oracle anticipates will come from outright savings on IT costs." Let's assume, for the moment, that the IT costs represent money spent. Most of the value will derive from increased productivity. The CFO explains: "If 80 percent of our 40,000 employees are customer-facing, and if we can boost their productivity 20 percent to 30 percent thanks to an integrated suite of web-enabled applications, that equals about $1.45 billion a year reaching the bottom line."

Benefit Inflation

The Oracle proclamations are examples of benefit inflation. Two billion dollars is certainly an impressive number. However, if the real savings are 13 percent of this, we're talking $260 million. This is not insignificant, of course, but it's not $2 billion. As is more often the case than not in my experience, companies claim to save, or promise to save, a significant amount of money when, in fact, they have not or will not save anything close to the value. Noncash costs have the same units as cash costs; they're all monetary units such as dollars. So, the $2 in savings from the improvement described in the baking example earlier appears the same as cash cost savings, since the unit of measure is dollars in both cases. There is nothing on the surface to distinguish this noncash savings from a true cash savings. This creates a challenge when we calculate the saving.

When we add the noncash savings to the cash savings, the total amount in dollars is higher than if we only considered cash savings. This is benefit inflation (Figure 2.2). Benefit inflation is real, and it is a significant issue. Go back to Oracle. Of the purported $2 billion in savings, a full $1.45 billion was noncash as mentioned previously, approximately 72 percent (Figure 2.3). The CFO mentioned the $1.45 would hit the bottom line, but how? Through increased sales? Increasing sales isn't savings, it's generating revenue. Did Oracle's sales increase by $1.45 billion due only to their software savings? Not likely. To achieve a $1.45 billion boost to the bottom line as the CFO promised, with a 77% gross margin and a

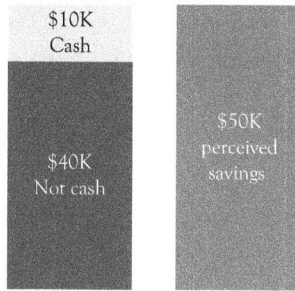

Figure 2.2 In many cases, value propositions are created with both cash and noncash elements. The noncash savings are the source of benefit inflation. They're often easy to create and large in scale

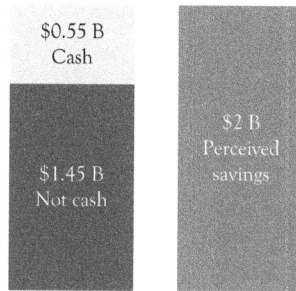

Figure 2.3 More than 72 percent of the savings promised by Oracle's CFO is not cash. Two billion dollars certainly sounds much more impressive than $0.5 billion. This is an extreme case of benefit inflation

Note: The math is inconsistent as per the CFO's comments. This figure represents the $1.45 billion in promised savings with the difference being cash. However, IT savings as laid out in the article would be $260 million not $550 million.

30% tax rate, Oracle customer facing people alone would have to create a marginal increase in sales of $2.69 billion over the organic growth the company was experiencing. The savings will certainly not come from the productivity increases that hit sales, general, and administrative (SGA) because if the people still work there and their salaries were not reduced, how would SGA change? In the end, one must question just how much money had been saved.

We learned early in life we can't do things like add apples and oranges. My ten-year-old son, to whom this book is dedicated, knows this. They're dissimilar. The same is still true when calculating the benefits from improvement projects. When we calculate savings, the calculations often include both cash and noncash costs due to the similar unit of measure and a lack of distinguishing whether the value is cash or not. When we do this, we are adding dissimilar things assuming they are the same. This violates a basic rule of arithmetic.

Let's go back to the $20 per hour laborer who is making loaves of bread. Assume we came up with a way to not only improve labor efficiency (10 loaves in an hour versus 5), but we can also buy cheaper materials; $8 for 10 pounds versus $10 for 10 pounds. The savings in material costs are real. We used to spend $10 and now we spend $8 for the same amount of material input. This is a savings of $2 per 10 pounds every time we buy flour. However, when considering total cost savings, this true cash savings is mixed with an artificial savings of $2 per unit in direct labor costs. This creates confusion regarding the source and extent of the cost savings and inflates the true savings. Consider Table 2.1.

Walking through this example, the company initially made 200 loaves of bread per week (five per hour over 40 hours). They spent $200 cash on materials and $800 cash on labor for the week. As the company increased output due to improved labor efficiency, the number of hours bought stayed the same, so the cash cost for labor is still $800. However, the increased output can only be sustained by buying more material, so the cash required for flour increases. We can see, then, that our cash costs have increased as a result of this improvement. However, there was supposed to be a cost reduction from being more efficient since labor costs have gone from $4 per unit to $2 per unit. Considering flour, the cost per loaf should have gone from $5 to $3, so the cost savings for producing 400 loaves should be $800. However, we do not see it directly, as cash leaving the organization, or cash$_{OUT}$, for the labor in both cases was the same.

This would suggest that there is not a cash savings from the efficiency improvement itself. The same amount is spent on labor in the first and second cases. As mentioned earlier in the chapter, this calculated noncash savings is one of the hard cost savings that is truly soft. When we reduced the labor cost per unit, we did not see a corresponding reduction in spend. As we will see later, the increased performance can lead to opportunities to make cash improvements but will not do so on its own accord.[11]

---

[11] Lee 2018.

Table 2.1 We can see the impact of cash and noncash costs by creating an example such as this and assessing how, when, and why cash flows out of the company

	Output/ week	Material cost per week	Labor cost per week	Cash spent per week	Labor cost per item	Aggregated cost savings per week	Cash savings per week
Initial	200 units	$200	800	$1000	$4	0	$0
Improve labor	400 units	$400	800	$1200	$2	$800	-$200
Improve materials	200 units	$160	800	$960	$4	$40	$40
Improve labor and materials	400 units	$320	800	$1120	$2	$880	$80

In the next scenario, we are looking at money spent on materials. To make 200 units, we initially paid $200 for flour. With the improvement in price, we now pay $160. We can see here there is a clear difference of $40; the company will spend $40 less per week on flour for the same output levels than they did previously. That is true cash savings.

Considering both improvements, we see that when the cash and noncash savings are combined, there is a pretty large improvement opportunity; $880. However, since the labor will not change, the only true cash savings is from the cost of materials. The improvement opportunity, as defined using the combination of cash and noncash costs, *is over 10 times larger* than the cash improvement opportunity in this case: $880 versus $80. This is benefit inflation. It's easy to see the excitement that the company might have, believing they have saved both material and labor costs. However, the only real savings from a cash perspective will be from materials. What is sad in this example is the likelihood that someone may be willing to buy services for $10 to save the artificial improvement of $800 but may turn down the opportunity to truly save $40 in cash because it is too small! The comparison one considers is 79:1 ROI for $800 to 3:1 for $40, although the 3:1 creates cash and the 79:1 does not. We can start seeing the importance of focusing on cash here. If we increase this by three orders of magnitude, it says folks would rather spend $10 thousand to save $800 thousand in noncash, but less likely to spend the money for a $40 thousand cash benefit.

Artificial savings are calculated frequently when determining the benefits of improvement projects. Without understanding the fact there are cash and noncash costs and without distinguishing between the two, benefit inflation will occur. And note, benefit inflation is often an indirect desire or manifestation of those selling the opportunity, whether it's an external vendor or an internal department head. The bigger the benefit opportunity, the greater the articulated ROI. This helps them build a stronger business case to move forward. The university director mentioned in Chapter 1 tried to inflate her benefits by not only including areas that would receive primary and secondary sources of benefit, but she also reached out to areas that may have been only remotely affected if at all. This led to a much higher articulation of benefits than would ever be realized by her project.

Lack of Clarity of the Path to Achieve Savings

True cash savings come from doing something; an act that affects the rate of cash$_{OUT}$. For instance, material savings in the previous example involved buying cheaper material. Sometimes, however, the act, corresponding details, and those responsible for acting are left out of the situation. The most common occurrences I've seen have been tied to "if-then" statements; *if we buy or implement X, then Y will happen.* For instance, if we buy this software, then inventory will go down; then costs will go down; then sales will go up. The question is, "How?" For inventory to go down, how, specifically, will this happen? Who is responsible for making it happen? What steps must occur for it to be true?

Oftentimes, consultants and others may use benchmarks, wild guesses or even resort to pulling estimates from the insides of their lower digestive track to create savings values. These numbers often have no factual basis that are tied to your specific company and details describing the path to achieving the benefit are left out. In many cases, the path to achieving the benefit is the most important criterion for achieving lasting, meaningful change.[12]

An example is the situation from Chapter 1 where $20 million in savings was promised by a consulting firm to a former customer. The question, of course, was, "How will this happen?" What will change so that the company will be spending $20 million fewer dollars? For this to occur from a cash perspective, practically the entire engineering staff would have had to be fired. For that to happen, someone would have to lead the effort to fire each engineer. There are risks, however. What if they do not release the engineer? If she still works there, the improvement has not led to her being a part of the anticipated cost savings. Had they thought through what might happen if engineers got word their jobs were going to be eliminated prematurely? What is the contingency plan for the work if the entire engineering department is let go, who is responsible for it, and when might it be executed? What would they have to pay in severance and when? There was no clear plan of action to achieve the

---

[12] C. Heath and D. Heath. 2010. "Switch: How to Change Things When Change Is Hard." *Broadway Books.*

$20 million and considering the previous example in the section on benefit inflation, our analysis of the $20 million in savings promised showed the true value proposition was about an order of magnitude off. In other words, the maximum cash value proposition was $2 million, being generous, versus the proposed $20 million.

The path to savings is one of the most important steps to value realization, yet the detailed plan telling us how to achieve value is often lacking or needs significant work, putting value realization, especially cash value realization, at risk.

Benefit Projection

Benefit articulation and value projection involves the following steps:

1. Clearly identify the benefits of the project, which are most often improvements in capacity efficiency as we will find later in the book
2. Determine the magnitude of the benefit from implementation and the management steps required to achieve the benefit,
3. Articulate the benefit in both timing and magnitude, and
4. Project the managerial activities, timing, and benefits to create a forecast or schedule of anticipated operations and cash improvements.

These steps serve three primary purposes. First, they will paint a picture of the opportunity available to the company, in time, effort, spend, resources required, and benefits. This summary will serve as a basis for understanding the project, what is possible, and where some of the risks associated with benefit suboptimization may be.

Second, we can look at the timing of cash outflows and inflows to assess when the expenditures and benefits will occur, and why. For instance, when we know the cash outflows, we can compare that with the timing of realizing benefits to determine if the timing is acceptable.

For one customer, the difference between spending money and the realization of benefit was much too long. The cash payback was 72 months. By looking at the chart highlighting the cash expenditures and savings and understanding the sources of both, we were able to break the project into manageable chunks in a way that somewhat mimicked an agile project by using pseudo scrums. We were able to identify smaller chunks with smaller investments and faster cash value realization. This shifted the risk of the project and ultimately made it self-funding.

The third purpose is to serve as a baseline for comparison during implementation. The project execution and management action will be based on the assumptions going into implementation. Once in the implementation phase, we will be able to compare actual value realization to projected value realization. This does a three things. First, it helps us understand whether we are ahead of, on, or behind schedule. Second, it helps us understand *why* we are where we are by comparing the assumptions and actions necessary to achieve the benefit to what happened. In other words, did the required, planned actions occur or not? If not, why not? Last, information from plan deviations can be captured in after action reviews for use in future projects.[13] This can range from assumptions being incorrect going into the project to improperly calculating the benefits to not properly considering or documenting the upside resulting from execution.

Benefits Realization

Two key considerations regarding benefit realization are execution with an emphasis on value realization and auditing the execution. The problem is, many don't do either, or they don't do them well. Oftentimes, the focus is on getting the projects approved. Once approved, it is often off to the next opportunity for leadership while the implementation team focuses on their work. Afterwards, the team is focused on project completion rather than value realization. For instance, the emphasis may be on getting the software up and running, which is an important step, but the specific activities involved with reducing the inventory to targeted levels may be compromised. This leaves a big opportunity hole for the company. Little or no benefit will be realized until the steps taken along the path to realizing benefit are executed. When the path, along with associated and necessary management action, does not exist or are poorly

---

[13] R.J. Baker. 2007. *Mind Over Matter: Why Intellectual Capital is the Chief Source of Wealth.* Wiley.

defined or poorly executed, realizable value is compromised. Of course, companies do execute because projects do get implemented. The questions are, "How effective were the plan and the path?"; "How effectively were they implemented?"; and possibly most importantly, "How much of the realizable value was actually realized?" We know this by comparing the value realized to the projected value as discussed previously. Sometimes this can be determined by looking at the financial statements. Going back to Oracle's $2 billion promise, when reviewing their financial statements, for instance, there was no definitive proof or obvious smoking gun that reflected the CFO's statement about value.

If benefits have been realized at the expected or an even greater rate, the questions are, "Why?" and "What can we learn from this for subsequent applications?" If you are behind projections, again, there are several questions such as, "Why?" "Were the benefits inflated?" "Were the assumptions not properly documented or handed off to the responsible parties effectively?" "Were the management actions not executed or did they fail?" All of these questions, both positive and negative, should be addressed in the after action review.

The second area is auditing the benefit realization. This is how we gain the information mentioned previously. The actual plan will vary from the projected plan for several reasons. As a result, it is imperative to review the execution plan so that actual benefit realization can be compared to projected. This will help identify both deficiencies with the implementation as well as unanticipated benefits. In the end, without purposefully auditing progress, comparing reality to projections, and looking to understand the variances, there is no assurance many, if any, of the anticipated benefits have, or will be realized. This is key information when implementing both the current project and when defining and implementing future projects.

The rest of the book will focus on both the process and the techniques. The objective is to provide you with tools that will help ensure greater cash ROI. Next chapter, I will focus on explaining why the traditional ways of financial value quantification limit, and sometimes even deter cash value realization, and how we can look at the process differently.

Key Takeaways

1. For the purpose of this book, realizing cash value is key. Accounting information is of little use at best, and is harmful at worse.
2. An effective, repeatable process must be in place for true cash value realization for all projects.
3. Companies must separate cash and noncash costs and savings and avoid combining them to inflate the benefit opportunity.
4. Oftentimes, implementing the project is not enough. There will be additional management action that is enabled by the improvement project, and it is this management action that will lead to cash value realization.

CHAPTER 3

Fundamentals of Cash Dynamics

An important objective of this book is to help define and identify the cash impact of improvement projects. Many attempt to use accounting tools and metrics to represent the cost of the project and the improvement benefit. This will not suffice. We need an approach that focuses on understanding and modeling cash dynamics and the factors that influence the flow of cash. Only by modeling cash effectively can we understand and manage the impact we have on cash with our improvement projects.

Before diving into the process of turning improvements into cash, we need critical context for thinking about and modeling cash. Practically everything in the methodology presented in this book revolves around one key objective: how do we ensure improvement projects make money for our firm? Of course, there are projects where making money is not the objective and that is fine. However, the purpose of *this* book is to help project teams and companies actually make money by creating a positive cash return on investment, or CROI, from the projects they implement.

Why do we need this context? Taken at face value, having an objective that cash-based improvement projects create more cash than was spent is a fairly benign notion. However, when we look under the covers, it's much more complicated.

Consider the cost of the improvement project. Let's say someone is estimating the cost of the project and they identify the need for a resource. They can either use an internal employee or an external resource. Assume the line item on a project budget for the person is for $20 thousand. If the "cost" is $20 thousand for the internal employee, but only $15 thousand for a similarly skilled outside resource, who would you pick? One may think it's better, from a profitability perspective, to go with the cheaper outside resource, as there is a significant difference between the two ($20 thousand versus $15 thousand), and you've already increased the profit by $5 thousand over what is budgeted. However, when considering cash spent by the organization, it's a no-brainer; $0 cash for the internal resource as discussed in Chapter 2 versus $15 thousand cash for the external.

The same thing happens when calculating benefits. Again, from Chapter 2, which is better, making a $100 thousand resource 10 percent more efficient resulting in $10 thousand in savings, or saving $7 thousand by buying lower priced materials? As discussed, making a salaried person more efficient doesn't change what they're paid, so the $10 thousand is not money. The $7 thousand bogey is a much more desirable target from a cash perspective. When the goal is cash and you're looking at the most appropriate data, these answers are obvious. The answers may not be intuitive to most, especially those who are vested in using accounting techniques to calculate savings, so let's take a deeper dive.

What I have found is that most savings calculations methodologies that I've seen are focused on calculating the monetary value of savings using accounting-based information. This is a mistake for two reasons. The first is that most accounting values such as costs and profits have nothing to do with money or cash.[1] The second is, many accounting numbers significantly skew monetary values in a way that misrepresents reality.

Consider making a salaried, or even hourly worker more efficient and claiming a cash savings. If there were cash savings from the $100 thousand employee mentioned above, we should see a reduction in money spent, but if she is still receiving the same salary, there will not be a transaction representing the $10 thousand reduction. This is a version of the calculation Oracle used, admittedly, for the $1.45 billion portion of its savings that it didn't realize.

---

[1] Lee 2016.

Let's think about product, service, a activity costs. Assume a company determines it costs them $3.75 to make a product. If that cost were money, we should see a transaction for $3.75 every time the company makes the product. They should save $3.75 when they don't. Do we see this? No. If it costs $35 to do a dental cleaning, do we see a cash transaction for every time a salaried hygienist does a cleaning? Does the dental office save $35 when she doesn't do a cleaning? No. When determined an activity such as processing an invoice costs $100, do we see a transaction for $100 every time an invoice is processed? No.

With the answer being "No" in each of these situations, think about cost savings; *if the costs do not represent cash, the savings that are based on them will not be cash.* Returning to the $3.75 product cost, if that's not money, reducing it to $3.25 from improvements will not lead to a 50¢ cash savings per unit.

Accounting does not deal with cash in this way and with this level of context. The closest accounting values to true cash are those found on the cash flow statement. Using the direct method where there are no accruals, the statement models cash. With the indirect method, however, accruals are involved, and whenever accruals are used, it's less certain. With cash flow statements, the information you get is *that* money was spent and not *how* or *why*. You know *that* you spent $100 thousand in labor last month, but that's it. You cannot look at that number and determine how many people you paid, what you paid them, or whether overtime was involved. In general, you may also not understand "why" you spent $100 thousand. You may normally spend $75 thousand per month, so is the extra $25 thousand overtime? Time and a half? Double time? Temporary laborers used to fill gaps in capacity? In other words, key context is lost, which limits the utility of the statements of cash flow as a managerial tool. Interestingly enough, even if the best cash information is found on the cash flow statements, one CEO confessed to me that he rarely looked at or used it.

Understanding the Dynamics of Cash

Making money is about cash transactions: money that comes in and leaves your company. Say, you wake up in the morning with $10 in your pocket, you make $7, and you spend $5 throughout the day. At the end of the day, you will have $12. You've made $2. This, itself, is another fairly benign notion. The key attributes are:

1. How much money did you start with ($10)?
2. How much money did you bring in ($7)?
3. How much money did you spend ($5)?
4. What was the time period (one day)?

The cash you end up with is equal to what you started the day with, plus what you received during the day, minus what you spent during the day.

This situation can be modeled with Equation 3.1 shown with the accompanying diagram in Figure 3.1.

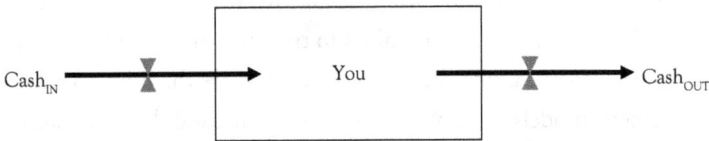

Figure 3.1 *If we put a box around you and measure how much cash you have at the beginning of a period, we will know how much cash you have at the end by measuring what cash flows in and out during the period*

$$cash_{END} = cash_{BEGINNING} + cash_{IN} - cash_{OUT} \qquad (Eq.\ 3.1)$$

Where,

$Cash_{END}$ is the cash at the end of the period;
$Cash_{BEGINNING}$ is the cash at the beginning of the period;
$Cash_{IN}$ is the cash that enters during the period;
$Cash_{OUT}$ is the cash that leaves during the period.

The same model works with organizations. We put a box called the Cash-In/Cash-Out or CiCo Border around the entire company and we look at $cash_{IN}$ and $cash_{OUT}$ over an analysis period. The difference between the two will tell us whether the company made or lost cash during the period (Figure 3.2). How much the organization has at the end of the

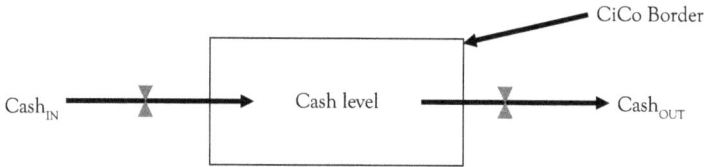

Figure 3.2 As with an individual, if we put a box around the company, we can understand how its cash changes over time, and we can predict and project cash values. The box we put around the company is called the cash$_{IN}$ cash$_{OUT}$ or CiCo Border. It must go around the entire company, not departments, divisions, cost centers, or profit centers

period is determined using Equation 3.1. Note, we do not need accounting profit and cost information to determine this.

As suggested, it is important to look at the entire organization and not, for instance, a department or a division. The reason is, a department can transfer cash from its budget to another department's budget. While the first department no longer has the money, no additional cash has left the organization as a result of the transfer, so nothing has changed regarding how much cash the organization has. This is why it costs the organization nothing for the $20 thousand resource mentioned previously. Although there may be a budget transfer within the organization, there is no cash impact. If, instead, the company spent money on an outside resource, that would affect cash$_{OUT}$ and lead to the organization being $15 thousand poorer as a result.

An example of this is found by considering a situation I once encountered with a previous employer. I was a professor at a school that had a shared services copy center. The school decided to charge departments for their copies, which makes sense on the surface. If we have a cost center, let's justify it by having folks pay for the products or services offered. The idea is, this should cover, or in some cases, justify the expense.

Let's say they decide to charge 5¢ for a copy. To our department, that is a cash cost because it leaves our budget when we buy copies. As a group looking to manage our own budget, it makes sense for us to consider cheaper alternatives. If we can find another source that offers to sell us copies for less money, say 3¢, it makes sense to us to go outside the organization to buy copies from that source.

From a departmental perspective, the decision made perfect sense. It's better to spend 3¢ rather than 5¢ for what is basically the same product. However, to the school, it's a very different story. We have now increased the cash cost to the organization. Why? Because we will still be paying for the shared services center; the labor, paying for the materials we've purchased, and the equipment we're buying or leasing. This money will be leaving regardless of whether they are making copies or not. So, when we decided to go outside to pay for copies, more money is leaving the school's coffers, resulting in a poorer cash position than if we had paid 5¢ for the copies (Figure 3.3).

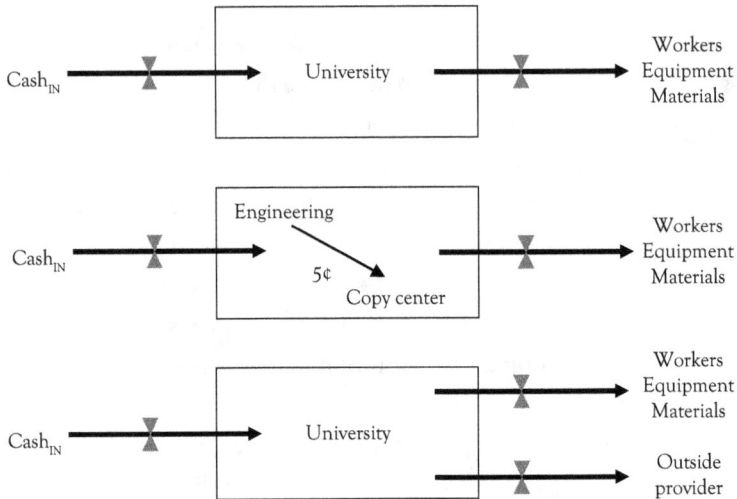

Figure 3.3 The focus should be on money that leaves the organization. If money does not leave, it does not affect cash. Buying copies internally had no impact on the school's cash, but spending outside did

Looking at the entire organization from a cash perspective rather than departments or divisions will help avoid this and similar scenarios, such as those involved with calculating the cost of the project. This will be a very important consideration when thinking about project costs and comparing internal to external resources.

Cash Improvements From Improvement Projects

We use the same cash dynamics concepts and equations to calculate the cash benefits of improvement projects. The amount of money the project makes is the difference between what the company spent to implement the project, reiterating, *money that left the organization due to spending not that allocated to the project*, and the cash improvement that is realized as a result of the implementation. The cash improvement, we will find, can either be an increased rate of cash coming in, or a relative decrease in the rate of cash going out. The analysis period generally starts when the project begins and lasts until the end of the value realization period, however that is defined.

Going back to Figure 3.2, when $cash_{IN}$ is greater than $cash_{OUT}$ over a period, the amount of cash the company has will increase. It's like water in a kitchen sink with $water_{IN}$ being greater than $water_{OUT}$. When more water comes in than leaves, the water level in the sink rises. If more water leaves than comes in, the water level declines. If the objective is to raise the water level in the sink, we have to ensure $water_{IN}$ is greater than $water_{OUT}$.

Similarly, the overall cash improvement must consider changes in both $cash_{IN}$ and $cash_{OUT}$. If the $cash_{IN}$ associated with realizing benefit is greater than $cash_{OUT}$ from the implementation, the amount of cash the organization has will increase (Equation 3.2). The total amount of the change is calculated using Equation 3.2, and this simple equation will be the source of understanding when, if, and how our projects create cash improvements. This is a very important point to consider. It is quite possible that projects with inflated benefits may cause $cash_{OUT}$ to be greater than $cash_{IN}$. Going back the scenarios from Chapter 1, in each case, the cash spent on consulting and software would have exceeded the cash benefits expected from the improvement, suggesting the companies would have lost, not gained cash.

$$\text{Cash improvement} = \Delta\ cash_{IN} - \Delta\ cash_{OUT} \qquad \text{(Eq. 3.2)}$$

Where,

$\Delta\ cash_{IN}$ looks at any changes in the rate which the company receives cash as a result of implementing the project;

$\Delta\ cash_{OUT}$ considers the rate at which the company spends cash on the project. This value includes all cash spent implementing the project and executing management activities necessary to realize the benefits.

Another useful metric is CROI. More traditional ROI, is also a significant metric for many companies. ROI is determined by taking the difference between anticipated savings and the cost to achieve these savings, or the investment, and dividing it by the investment (Equation 3.3). For instance, if you spend $1,000 and the improvement is $6,000, the ROI is 5:1 ($6,000 – $1,000) ÷ $1,000.

$$ROI = (savings - investment) \div investment$$

$$Cash\ ROI = cash\ improvement \div investment \qquad (Eq.\ 3.3)$$

$$Cash\ ROI = (\Delta\ cash_{IN} - \Delta\ cash_{OUT}) \div cash_{Investment}$$

What is more important here is CROI. In this case, we are looking at the cash spent and the resulting improvement in cash. This means for CROI, we must look only at money entering and leaving the company. Efficiency savings, for example, would not be considered because they are not cash. Costs associated with the use of internal resources, too, will not factor in. As such, CROI tends to be smaller in cases involving using external resources because the investment is larger. However, with smaller investments from internal resources, the CROI may actually be higher, which is an important note. To illustrate, with the previous example, assume $750 of the $1,000 was tied to the value of an internal employee. If you receive the $6,000 benefit while spending $250, the CROI is actually 23:1 versus 5:1 if everything else remained the same.

All of this should seem straightforward. It if does, great. Now, let's rock the boat a bit. Much of the information about savings and costs that is used in ROI calculations, we get from accounting information, tools and approaches. The problem is, accounting information, specifically cost and managerial accounting information, doesn't give us what we think it gives us. It does not give us the cash information that we need to understand and calculate benefits and to calculate CROI.[2] Consider a $120 thousand IT employee we are considering putting on our project.

---

[2] Ibid.

How do we calculate the cost of her time? Let's say a project will improve her efficiency. How much money is being saved as a result? Although accounting can provide answers, they are neither cash oriented nor are the calculated values unique. Let's consider each.

Not Cash Oriented

For the cash equation, Equation 3.1 to work, we need boundaries to allow us to measure the rate of $cash_{IN}$ and $cash_{OUT}$. This is the CiCo Border mentioned previously and shown in Figure 3.2. Inside this border is the amount of money, cash, the company has at any given point in time. This is the cash level. If we measure $cash_{IN}$ and $cash_{OUT}$ of the box over time, we will know if, during a given period of time, the cash level increases or decreases. Cash coming in and leaving the organization are the only ways the cash level can be affected.

Accounting values do not necessarily reflect cash transactions, and most are, in fact, not cash at all. Consider accounting costs. They are simply opinions of value and nothing more.[3] That's a pretty strong statement. Let's consider a simple cost and benefit scenario to demonstrate. Our IT employee is paid a salary of $120K per year. You want three weeks of her time on a project. How do you figure out the "cost" to have her on your project for budgeting purposes? Somehow, you need to convert the annual salary to three weeks, but how? Let's say you divide $120K by 52. That's approximately $2,300 per week. Every week she is on the project "costs" the company $2,300—or does it? You are paying her a salary, so the company does not see an increase of $2,300 in $cash_{OUT}$ for every week she works on your project. There is no company level $2,300 cash transaction for her time. In fact, as suggested previously, it costs the company nothing from a cash perspective for her to work with you.

You may or may not choose to backfill her position. The management issue you face is that by using her for three weeks, she isn't available during that time to do her regularly assigned tasks. If you choose to backfill and you do so with a person you hired from the outside, that act of hiring someone from the outside and paying them a salary is where the

---

[3] Lee 2018.

cash$_{OUT}$ increases. Otherwise, you can assign her to the project, choose not to backfill, and not have the associated increase in cash$_{OUT}$. In any case, the $2,300 per week for her time, itself, is not a cash cost. Instead, it represents what we believe is a reasonable value of a week of her time, and that is what often gets used for budgeting purposes.

The same holds true for benefits. Let's say a task takes a person making $60,000 one hour. With the improvement, the person will now take 20 minutes to perform the same task. How much is saved? Assuming we use a 2,000-hour work year, we calculate a cost of $30 per hour as an hourly rate. Hence, we determine the task "costs" $30. With the improvement, we have unquestionably saved 40 minutes in time. However, one would be tempted to argue we have saved $20 since the task used to *cost* $30 and now *costs* $10. When looking at the cash level, cash$_{OUT}$ has not changed, so no cash was saved. Hence, the $20 is a value placed on the 40 minutes saved.

These cost and savings calculations are dangerous. On the cost side, it causes project managers and leaders to make bad choices in the name of managing their project's profitability. We saw this previously on the cost side when comparing the $20 thousand internal resource to the $15 thousand external resource. On the benefit side, we have benefit inflation as we saw with Oracle. The consultant comes along and says, "Your department budget is $10M. If our software can make your department just 10 percent more efficient, we will save you $1M." No, you won't. These benefit calculations are not true from a cash perspective.

Not Unique

Let's go back to the IT employee's cost to our project. I proposed this is not a cost but, instead, an opinion of value. We chose to take her salary and divide it by 52 weeks to calculate a cost per week of $2,300. However, what if, instead, we decided to consider her three weeks of vacation? She's really only being paid to work 49 weeks, so should we consider 49 versus 52 weeks? If we do, now her cost per week is $2,450. If we take out our 15 paid holidays, she's now only working 46 weeks, so the cost per week has gone up to $2,600. We do this all, however, to determine what one week is worth.

The costs we calculated are tied to the assumptions we make and to arbitrary math. The assumptions we make are subjective. Do we choose holidays or not? Do we choose vacation time or not? These are subjective choices. It is this subjectivity associated with the choices that leads me to describe costs as opinions of value. Opinions led to the parameters chosen and used to define value. There is also the question of which approach one chooses to calculate costs. Should one use activity-based costing? Another approach? If so, which one? The choice of approach, too, is subjective.

Regarding the arbitrary relationships, consider this. The cash cost to a company does not change based on the work an employee does for it. The employee gets paid $120K per year or $10K per month regardless of what work she does. So, whether she is on a project 0 weeks or all 52, her salary does not change (Figure 3.4).

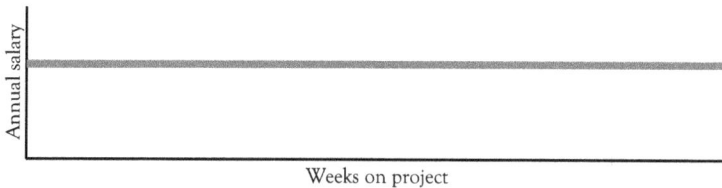

Figure 3.4 *Although a simple chart, the idea is powerful. The labor you buy and how you use them are unrelated from a cash perspective*

When you buy capacity, what you pay for the capacity and how you use it are unrelated from a cash perspective. This suggests that what she is paid and what she does during the year are mathematically independent. There is no relationship between the two. None. Want proof? Does your salary change based on the work you do? No. Even if you're commission-based, you only get commission when the customer buys what you're selling, and the transaction meets the requirements of your company. The work leading up to it does not change your salary.

Since there is no relationship between her pay and the number of weeks she is on a project, to create a cost per week involves making up a mathematical relationship between two things that are mathematically independent of one another. When you do this, the mathematical relationship is arbitrary. For example, you can create a relationship between the number of houses in your neighborhood and the number of planes that fly over the neighborhood during the course of a day, but that number has no mathematical relevance. It's not as if another 3.8 houses will somehow pop up if one more plane is diverted over your neighborhood. The relationship means nothing. In the case of the worker, you can divide her salary by 52, 49, 46, or any number of weeks you want, but it won't represent cash and no single value is any more correct or valid mathematically than the other. And regardless, if she works another week on a project, the company isn't going to be out another $2,300, $2,450, or $2,600 as a result.

Another challenge this creates is determining just how much accounting cost was saved. Consider a $60K per year employee. As with our IT resource, depending on how we calculated the hourly cost for the $60K per year employee, the savings will change. We know we saved 40 minutes of her time, but what is this in terms of value? Is it $20 (2K hours per year), $19.23 (52 weeks and 40 hours/week), $22 (46 weeks and 40 hours per week) or $19.32 (46 weeks and 45 hours/week)? The issue for leaders looking for accounting value isn't the reality that 40 minutes saved. Instead, the issue is about how we choose to represent the value of the 40 minutes

These factors create significant challenges when trying to understand the impact of improving an organization's performance using accounting information. There should be a way to have an unambiguous approach to describe, model, and quantify the impact of improvement projects. That is the topic of the next chapter.

Key Takeaways

1. When improvement projects are about generating cash, accounting information will not work. You must use a cash-based analysis and avoid accounting costs and accounting profit.

2. Cash can only be affected by money that comes into and leaves an organization over the same period. Efficiency usually has no effect on cash savings because it doesn't affect the rate of cash leaving the company.

3. When considering both cash costs and benefits, focus on how the rate of change of cash is affected. That way you will be able to project the cash impact of both the project cost and the project's benefits.

CHAPTER 4

Introduction to Business Domain Management

One way to look at a business is to break it down into two parts or domains using the Business Domain Management framework. The two parts are 1. where decisions, actions, and commitments occur, and 2. how we describe what happened from a financial perspective for reporting purposes. Where the business activity happens is the operations and cash or OC Domain. The reporting happens in the Accounting Domain. Our improvement projects will affect what happens in the OC Domain, so this is where we should focus our efforts.

In the last chapter, I focused on two things. First, to understand cash, what affects cash, and to understand improvements to cash, we have to model cash. Unfortunately, most companies do not. They rely on accounting information instead. Second, accounting does a poor job modeling cash and providing the context we need to improve cash, so we should not use it as a tool for managing project costs and benefits.

To address these and other factors I propose the use of Business Domain Management, or BDM. BDM can be used to model an organization, its performance, and to provide insight into how we affect and manage operations and cash performance through improvement projects and other managerial activities. BDM is a business framework that was designed to create a direct relationship between operations, cash, and accounting, and show the direct impact, or lack thereof, of improvement projects and management action on both cash and accounting values.[1] It focuses on cash and the factors that affect cash, while demonstrating why saving on accounting costs often have no, and sometimes even negative effects on cash.

BDM starts by breaking organizations down into two business domains, the Operations and Cash, or OC Domain, and the Accounting Domain (Figure 4.1). This will allow us to model and understand what happens, why, and where in an organization with the proper context. Some of the information will be straightforward, such as understanding where business transactions occur. However, some of it isn't, such as where cash data comes from and where we should model it. Each domain will be discussed in turn.

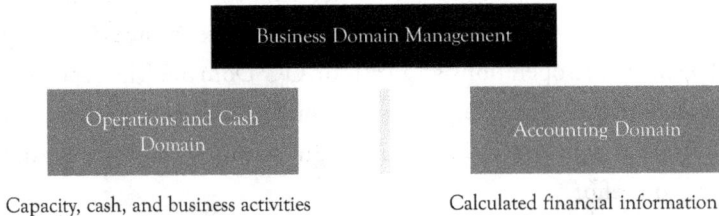

Business Domain Management

Operations and Cash Domain

Accounting Domain

Capacity, cash, and business activities   Calculated financial information

Figure 4.1 Businesses can be broken down into two domains, the Operations and Cash Domain and the Accounting Domain. They are separate and distinct, and it's important to understand what activities, data, and information reside in both

The OC Domain

The OC Domain reflects where business activities and cash transactions occur. It begins with the cash model from Figure 3.2, which is repeated here as Figure 4.2. Consider $cash_{IN}$ and $cash_{OUT}$. $Cash_{IN}$ represents cash received. For the most part, cash is received because something was sold, and cash was received for the sale. However, that's not the only way. The infusion of cash from lending sources, royalties, and licensing fees received are examples of other sources of $cash_{IN}$.

Regarding $cash_{OUT}$, cash leaves the company generally because we are paying for something we bought. Most of what we buy is capacity, what we

---

[1] Ibid.

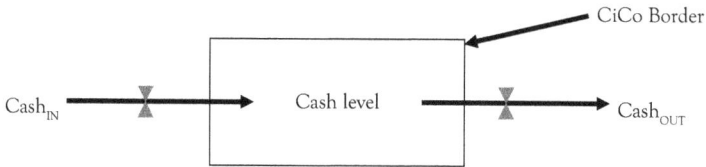

Figure 4.2 Only activities and activities in the OC Domain affect cash entering, and living the company

buy in anticipation of use.[2] For instance, you have workers, and you pay them expecting you will use them to do work. You lease space expecting you will need it for work or to store things. You buy materials expecting you will use them for work or to convert into salable items. However, it's not always things we buy because payments such as taxes, royalties owed, dividends, and fines are not necessarily tied to things we bought.

There are five primary capacity types: space, labor, equipment, materials, and information technology.[3] They all have the same basic characteristics. You buy a certain amount, you pay for what you buy, you consume what you bought, and you create output of all sorts (Figure 4.3). For instance, we buy time, space, equipment, and materials to make widgets

Figure 4.3 These are the primary business activities that occur in the OC Domain

---

[2] R.T. Yu-Lee. 2002. "Essentials of Capacity Management." *John Wiley & Sons.* Note, in the book, there were five entities. However, with the advent of online models where companies subscribe to IT, IT hardware can be considered equipment.

[3] Ibid.

that we sell in the market. In some cases, what you create, you can sell, but not all. For instance, we buy the labor that comprises our HR department. One source of their output is hired employees, but we don't sell hired employees. Or we buy a day of someone's time, we buy access to the space they'll work in, and the computers they will use, we consume each, and we create data analytics reports.

Notionally, all business operations can be modeled by looking at how much capacity there is, how it is consumed, and what it creates. Most of what we will use to understand the impact of improvement projects throughout the rest of the book is based on this model.

As mentioned previously, the capacity you buy and pay for affects $cash_{OUT}$ and what you sell and receive payment for affects $cash_{IN}$. From this interaction, you can create a comprehensive model of operations and the resulting cash transactions. This is the OC Domain's Business Activity Framework.[4] It models all business operations activities and cash transactions (Figure 4.4).

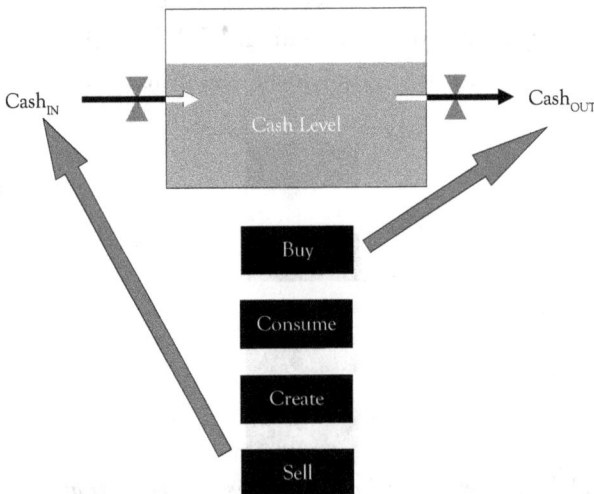

Figure 4.4 The Business Activity Framework models business activities and cash transactions and shows the relationship between business activities and how they affect cash transactions

---

[4] Lee 2018.

For instance, let's say you have a person who makes $25 per hour. For a shift, they will be paid $200. Let's assume seven hours were consumed on productive activities, and from this, 56 units of output were created and 48 were sold at a price of $8 each.

This scenario is modeled in Figure 4.5. The diagram is called a capacity map, and we use capacity maps to represent Buy-Consume-Create, or BCC activities discussed previously.

| 8 hours | 7 hours | 56 | 48 |
| Buy | Consume | Create | Sold |

Figure 4.5 This is a typical capacity map, which represents capacity purchased, consumed, and used to create output – Buy-Consume-Create. None of this information is contained in the Accounting Domain. Another key factor is demand. Demand is not found in the Accounting Domain. We only see the influence of demand met

From this simple example, a significant amount of both operational and financial information can be captured as seen in Table 4.1. I often hear from executives and consultants alike that they need the accounting information for managerial decisions and cannot shift to another set of data and information. The question is, "Why?" This information, created in the OC Domain, is the source of what is created in the Accounting Domain. The Accounting Domain, as we will see later, does not add anything, it just processes and creates one of what is practically an infinite number of descriptions of what has already happened in the OC Domain.

In this case, we know revenue generated, cash spent, and we have a significant number of metrics that help us understand where we have too much capacity, and what is necessary to achieve various types of improvements. We can see very clearly what the cash implications would be, given certain changes in operations and capacity levels. But then someone comes along and asks what the output, 56 units costs, and what the subsequent profit is.

This simple question, "What does it cost?" opens up Pandora's box. Why? The question is mathematically impossible to answer from a cash perspective and needs another solution. Let's consider why and discuss the relevance to projects.

Table 4.1 I often hear people tell me they cannot shift away from Accounting Domain information. Why can't they? First, all the information you need to manage is created in the OC Domain. Nothing new is created in the Accounting Domain. Second, where do they think the data they use come from?

Revenue (cash$_{IN}$)	$384
Costs (cash$_{OUT}$)	$200
Δcash	$184
Gross efficiency (output ÷ total capacity)	56 units ÷ 8 hours = 7 units/hour
Net efficiency (output ÷ productive capacity)	56 units ÷ 7 hours = 8 units/hour
Utilization	7 ÷ 8 = 76%
Productivity	(56 − 48) ÷ 48 = 1/6 or 17% overproductive
Nonproductive time	1 hour
Capacity required to meet demand	6 hours (two less than purchased)
If we buy 6 hours and aligned output with demand	
Revenue (cash$_{IN}$)	$384
Costs (cash$_{OUT}$)	$150
Δcash	$234
Gross efficiency = Net efficiency	48 units ÷ 6 hours = 8 units/hour
If we could figure out how to get 48 units buying 5 hours of labor through improvements	
Revenue (cash$_{IN}$)	$384
Costs (cash$_{OUT}$)	$125
Δcash	$259
Gross efficiency = Net efficiency	9.6 units/hour

First, let's consider a simple example we're all familiar with to drive this notion home. Let's say you buy phone service where you pay $25 for unlimited local calls. Long-distance calls are 10¢ per minute. A 10-minute long distance call would cost $1. How much would a 10-minute local cost? No clear answer, right? Here's why. When you made the long-distance call, you were buying time; a minute for 10¢. The cash cost curve looks like the one found in Figure 4.6A. With the local calls, you are buying access. This cost is the same whether you make 0, 10, 50, or an infinite number of calls. That cost curve looks like the one in Figure 4.6B. Recall, this is the same curve we created with our IT employee in Figure 3.4. These costs change with how much we buy and what we pay

Cash paid, or to be paid, is directly influenced by the length of the long distance call. Hence, there is a dependent relationship between the cost and the length.

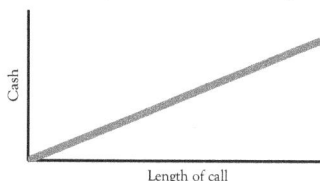

With local calls, there is no relationship between the calls you make and what you pay. Hence, the two are mathematically independent.

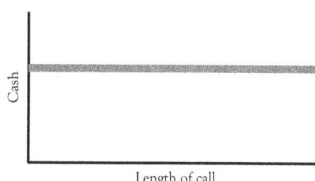

Figures 4.6A and 4.6B Cash costs change with what we buy. Noncash costs change with what we do. Mathematically, there is no relationship between what we buy, access for a period, and how we use it, making calls. This is the mathematical dilemma accounting tries, and fails, to address

for them. This suggests that there is no relationship between what you bought, access for $25, and how you use it making calls. However, to calculate a cost, you need a relationship. If you need one and you don't have one, you make it up. Enter accounting and the Accounting Domain.

The Accounting Domain

The Accounting Domain exists primarily for financial reporting purposes. It also exists to address accounting-related questions related to costs, profit, taxes, and other financial matters. These are values that cannot be calculated in the OC Domain because to calculate them requires a transformation of the OC Domain data. The OC Domain provides raw unambiguous data about the operations and cash transactions of a company, and that's it. To create accounting information, we take data from the OC Domain and use a transformation algorithm to turn into accounting information such as cost and profit (Figure 4.7).

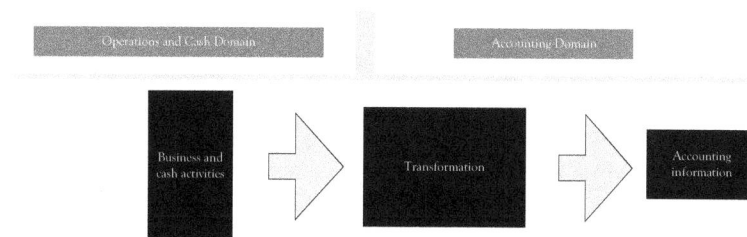

Figure 4.7 Accounting information comes from transforming business and cash activity data from the OC Domain

Calculating a cost in this example will require identifying the appropriate OC Domain data (what we paid and length of call) and transforming it into a cost (cost per 10 minute call). In other words, you need to somehow transform what you pay for a month of phone access $25 to the length of the call, 10 minutes. But how? It turns out, the same way we handled labor earlier on project costs and savings; we make it up. One way is to calculate a *per minute* rate, but how? What do you use? Do you use the total number of minutes in a month? If so, are you willing to accept February is the most expensive month to make phone calls solely because it has fewer minutes? Or that months with 30 days have more expensive calls than those with 31? Should we consider a 24-hour day or the time we'd likely be making calls, say, 16 hours per day ... or is it 17, 15, 20, or 8? That is the subjectivity of calculating costs. In the end, whatever model you use is arbitrary because you are still creating a relationship between mathematically independent values.

As a result, the cost of the local call can be whatever you want it to be, really, within certain parameters. For instance, the cost of a call can't exceed $25. If you have a cost per minute of $2, someone calls you and hangs up, say, in 0.05 seconds, the cost of that call could be calculated to be $40 even though you spent $25 for access. That makes no sense. Other than that, it's pretty much all fair game. Here's what's going on.

Business activity and cash transactions occur in OC Domain. Calculated costs and accounting information exist in the Accounting Domain. The Accounting Domain is the result of a transformation of OC Domain data into accounting information (Figure 4.8). The transformation is

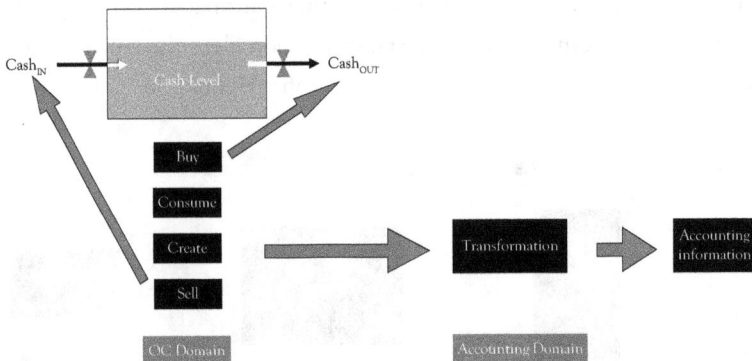

Figure 4.8 The Business Domain Management framework includes both the OC Domain and the Accounting Domain

necessary because there is no relationship between what you bought, capacity, and how you use it, but to calculate a cost, a relationship must be created. Hence, we take data from the OC Domain and transform it into information that can answer accounting questions.

The transformation process involves defining a data scope in the OC Domain and using a transformation algorithm to create an Accounting Domain image of what happened in the OC Domain. For example, take the person who makes $25 per hour. We know what we bought (eight hours for $200), we know what was consumed (seven hours), and what was created in that time (56 units). One way to calculate a cost per unit is to take the total time and cost ($200) and divide it by output to calculate an image or cost of $3.57. However, a different scope and set of assumptions will create a different image or cost (Figure 4.9). For instance, if we choose to use the seven productive hours instead of the eight total hours with the same output, the cost is $3.13.

Notice two things here. First, we have two costs in the Accounting Domain with only one set of OC Domain data. In other words, nothing

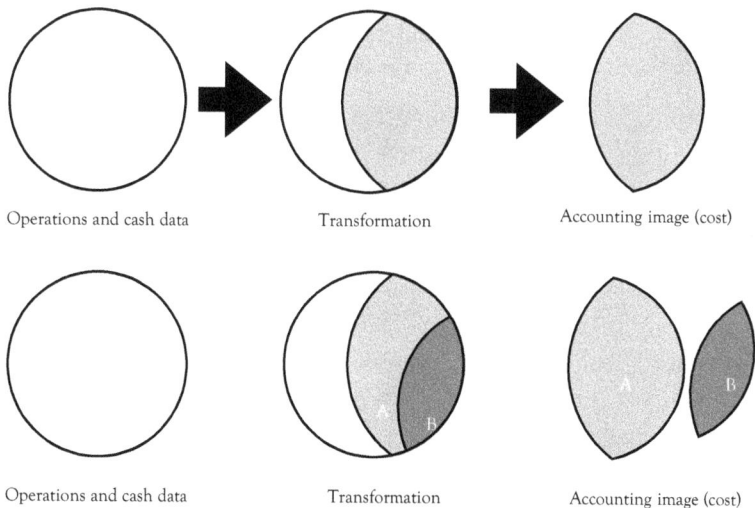

| Operations and cash data | Transformation | Accounting image (cost) |

| Operations and cash data | Transformation | Accounting image (cost) |

Figure 4.9 There is only one instance of operations and cash data. However, there are practically an infinite number of ways to transform it into accounting image. The lack of convergence to a single image is one of several reasons why business value should not be placed in accounting information

changed in the OC Domain, yet by changing the assumptions and, hence, the transformation algorithm, we came up with a cost that is arguably significantly different. Second, these are just two of a practically infinite number of possible costs. We could change the scope to consider how long each unit takes to make, how we classify production time, and many other factors. We can also change the transformation technique. We used average costing, but that could as easily have been a different costing approach such as standard, activity based, lean, or something else. Each will create its own unique cost (Figure 4.10).

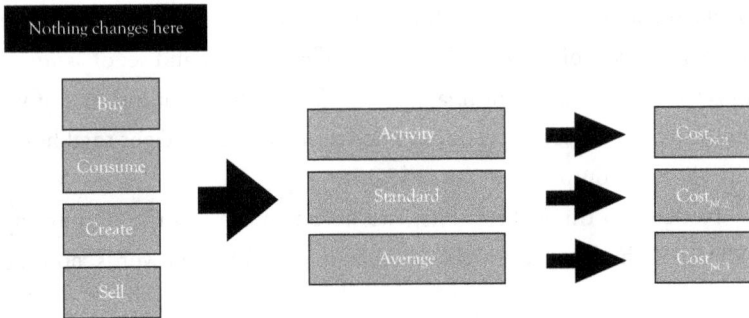

Figure 4.10 *We see that, although nothing changes in the OC Domain, how you choose to calculate costs affects what the cost becomes. Note, Cost$_{NCX}$ refers to noncash costs that are calculated from each transformation*

Why is this significant? If we look at the transformation process, OC Domain data are concrete, real data. However, Accounting Domain information is an abstraction of the real data that exists in the OC Domain. In fact, it's not just one abstraction. There are an infinite number of them. Hence, while you may have one you are working with and using for managerial decisions, it would be easy for someone to come along and create a completely different, equally valid (or not) abstraction with a different cost and profit from the exact same OC Domain data. If that's the case, how do you know if your information is any better?

Project financial analyses and CBAs are often captured or modeled in the Accounting Domain. Think about the cost reduction we discussed earlier when we reduced processing time for the employee from one hour to 20 minutes, and the different ways we could calculate the savings.

When we considered the cost of internal resources, that is Accounting Domain information. Likewise, financial benefit calculations that result from improvements in efficiency, for instance, are also in the Accounting Domain. Because of the ambiguity of the information in the Accounting Domain and the fact that it is transformed or processed OC data, the proposal here is that if you want concrete, accurate, precise, data and information, you should model projects using OC Domain data rather than Accounting Domain information.

We can always project OC Domain data into the Accounting Domain to see what the impact will be on Accounting Domain information and metrics. However, this is much harder, if not practically impossible to project Accounting Domain data into the OC Domain and create managerially useful information.[5] For example, consider a product or service your company provides. Now say something happened that reduced that cost by 10¢. With this information, can you describe what happened in the OC Domain? No. Was there a change to how much capacity you bought or the price of the capacity? Was it based on capacity consumption rates? Improvement in terms of output that can be created in the same time? The answer is, from this information alone, we do not know. By focusing on the OC Domain, we are dealing with clean operations and cash data. If we make a change to the BCC Model, we can project the impact in the Accounting Domain. In other words, we can see where the 10¢ improvement came from. We will see later, why focusing on the OC Domain versus the Accounting Domain is so much more effective when modeling projects.

Next, we will focus on the importance of defining and prioritizing projects to ensure that they are able to generate cash returns for the firm as defined in the OC Domain, and that they're aligned with both the strategy of the firm and the needs of your customers.

Key Takeaways

1. Organizations can be broken down into two business domains, the Operations and Cash or OC Domain, and the Accounting Domain.

---

[5] Ibid.

2. The OC Domain is where we have true cash data. We understand not only what came into, and left the organization, but also why. This is critical for managerial decision making.

3. Information from the Accounting Domain is subjectively and arbitrarily contrived. Any set of Accounting Domain information is one of many possible representations of what truly happened in the OC Domain.

4. As such, since the Accounting Domain is an abstraction of the OC Domain, we should model business activities in the OC Domain where we have a concrete understanding of business activities and transactions. This will allow us to have a more comprehensive understanding of how the organization will change operationally, and what, specifically, needs to happen to ensure that cash benefits will occur from improvement projects.

CHAPTER 5

The Project Selection and Value Realization Process

An effective project selection process can set the tone for strategic alignment and value realization. Certain types of projects align with strategy more effectively than others. Some projects are not designed for cash value realization. It's important to have a framework that will help define both project type and its alignment to strategy so that projects can be prioritized effectively and selected appropriately.

This book is about realizing cash value from your improvement projects. The first step in the process of value realization is selecting and prioritizing projects. Companies have limits—limited budgets, time, people, and limits to the amount of change they can absorb. As a result, companies do not have the luxury of implementing every project that seems interesting or valuable at any time they want. They must choose, and to do so, they will need a prioritization approach.

When dealing with companies of all sizes, from start-ups to some of the largest and most successful companies in the world, rarely have I seen an effective approach that allows leaders to prioritize a portfolio of improvement opportunities or projects based on two key criteria; strategic relevance and the ability to achieve desired cash value from the project based on project type.

Oftentimes, a process may be broken, so there is an improvement project designed to fix it. There may be an area that may be considered high cost by consultants and subsequently deemed in need of improvement. Sometimes, a company thinks something is wrong and may not be sure exactly what it is, so they need to figure out what is wrong and how to fix it. In each of these cases, the project is often considered in the context of the extent to which the process is perceived as being broken, and the value associated with fixing it, but not necessarily in terms of the type of project being considered and its strategic relevance.

This is a problem. According to Peter Keen, author of *The Process Edge*, "firms have invested in processes that were not critical to their success. Processes were improved, sometimes dramatically, but they were not the salient ones. Key processes went on unexamined, some even suffering from the attention given to less important ones, so the change program succeeded but the firm succumbed."[1] Leaders need an objective way to identify and prioritize those processes that are strategically important to the company and its cash generation potential while also allowing leaders to compare and prioritize project options based on these factors.

One approach involves creating a Project Prioritization Matrix that considers both salience and project type. This matrix is a hybrid that comes from two sources: Peter Keen's Salience Worth Matrix from *The Process Edge*[2] and sage advice offered early in my career.[3] The Project Prioritization Matrix, pictured in Table 5.1, creates a built-in prioritization schema that helps determine which projects should be approved and in what order based on salience and anticipated cash returns. Let's look at the two axes on the matrix.

Table 5.1 The Project Prioritization Matrix helps categorize projects based on the salience of the process being improved and the type of project being purchased

	Informational	Instructional	Implement
Identity			
Priority			
Background			
Mandated			

---

[1] P.G.W. Keen. 1997. *The Process Edge: Creating Value Where It Counts*, 16. Harvard Business Review Press.

[2] Ibid.

[3] Do not know the source, unfortunately.

Project Salience

In his book, the *Process Edge*, Peter Keen creates an intriguing model that focuses on the notion of process salience or visibility. According to Keen,

> The word salience suggests standing out from the general surface, being prominent; salient processes are the most prominent ones. They are the processes that relate most directly to the firm's identity—those that visibly differentiate it from its competitors—and the priority activities that keep the engine of everyday competitive performance running.[4]

The idea is that processes that are more salient in the eyes of customers or the market may have a greater strategic importance or value to your company. However, part of the issue is, companies often do not take salience into consideration when considering improvement projects, so opportunities to enhance this relationship are often lost.

Keen defines four types of processes: identity, priority, background, and mandated in order of salience.[5]

Identity processes define a company to itself, its customers, and its investors. For FedEx, Keen mentioned, it's their reliability. The process of delivering packages to our home or work is what we largely know them for. The delivery process is likely the most salient process to their customer base: those who engage them and pay the bills. For McDonalds, it's their speedy consistent food preparation and their loyalty.[6]

Priority processes are "the engine of corporate effectiveness" and they provide the greatest level of support to the company and its identity processes. For instance, with FedEx, priority processes might include information technology and the ability to track packages on a real-time basis, the route planning process that maximizes coverage while minimizing fuel cost and travel times, and the logistics network of trucks and airplanes that help ensure the packages get to the warehouses before they go out

---

[4] Ibid, 16.
[5] Ibid, 26.
[6] Ibid.

for delivery. These are processes that are important when delivering the reliability we expect, but they, themselves, are not what FedEx is known for. For McDonalds, it may be food supply management, as McDonalds is a restaurant not a food distributor.[7] However, the food supply management process helps enable the consistency the market looks for. The idea behind priority processes is, if they fail, the identity processes, too, may fail. Hence, there is an elevated importance that priority processes have over the next type of process, background processes.

Background processes are the other processes that enable a business to operate effectively. For the most part, they are the processes that are not identity or priority. For FedEx and McDonalds, for instance, accounts payable or payroll may be background processes. This isn't to suggest they aren't important processes. On the contrary, they are very important. However, neither payables nor payroll defines either company. They are critical processes that needs to operate effectively.

A natural inclination is to identify types of processes automatically as being an identity, priority, or background process. This isn't the case. HR may be a background process for a hospital, but for a consulting firm or a company that offers staffing services, HR may be a priority process. Each determination should be aligned with the company's strategy, brand, and offerings rather than generically assigning categories to processes.

The fourth type of process is a *mandated process*. Mandated processes are either those that are required by the government, are required to meet government rules and regulations such as taxes and reporting, and those required by clients or other agencies. These processes are directly tied to some sort of compliance issue, contract, or other requirement. The key here is, the process is a requirement and needs attention. Where it falls on the prioritization scale is likely best considered on a situation-by-situation basis. Considerations should include the importance of inaction (nothing, fine, or imprisonment), and, hence, the penalties for noncompliance should be salient in the assessment itself.

---

[7] Ibid.

Project Type

The next axis focuses on the type of projects that are being considered. Early in my career, someone told me people buy or execute three types of projects:

- Informational
- Instructional
- Implementation

Informational

Informational projects focus on providing information about a problem the company may be facing. Often, this involves strategic or tactical situations where the company is trying to understand whether there is an issue, what to do about it, and to gain guidance about the impact of fixing it, or not. Common among informational projects is assessments, risk analyses, and strategy design sessions. Key for these engagements is to highlight performance challenges and issues and recommend a course of action. What you have at the end of this type of an engagement is often a presentation of facts, figures, findings, recommendations, and sometimes anecdotes that help explain what is going on, why, what the company should do, and the expected outcome as a result of following the recommendations.

Instructional

There will be a point where companies know what they need to do. They understand they need to reduce costs, for instance, but how? They know they need to offer new, or cut existing products or services, or to create a new division. How should they move forward? What's the plan?

Instructional projects focus on instructing the company how to move forward by creating a plan to address the issues found in the informational projects. Included in this should be the scope of the project, objectives, high level-to-detailed level project plan, expected benefits and costs when reasonable to estimate them, and ideally, a governance plan to ensure tasks are carried out to achieve the projected benefits.

Until this point, we have gotten information; we know what is wrong and we have a plan to execute so that we can improve our performance. Information and instruction are valuable, of course, but their value is limited to their ability to be implemented.

Implementation

Implementation involves executing the plan described in the output from an instructional project. This means buying and implementing the software, hiring three new salespeople, implementing lean, or shutting down the division. This is where the rubber meets the road. Promised efficiency improvements will not happen completely without implementing the software that enables them. Sales increases will not happen without adding the extra staff that will pound the pavement to create opportunities with new or existing customers.

The idea is, when it comes to the prioritization of projects in the context of creating cash value, one would generally prefer projects that involve implementation over providing information or instruction. Informational and instructional projects have no financial value to them on their own. The purpose they serve is tied to the promise of savings, both positive and negative, that will result from implementation. If the promise of savings is positive and it makes sense to move ahead, the information has been valuable. However, if the savings potential is negative, knowing this, too, is positive.

The Project Prioritization Matrix allows you to plot each project opportunity based on salience and project type and use this as a basis for prioritizing your project portfolio.

Interpreting the Chart

There is no single way to assess or interpret the data from the chart. Much of it is a function of where you are as a company. Consider project type. The initial thought might be that implementation projects are the most important and, therefore, should have priority over others. However, this may not always be the case. There are three factors I've seen that influence the general prioritization schema or approach:

1. Where is the company in terms of need?
2. What is the lead time to value realization?
3. What is the size of the opportunity?

Where Is the Company?

The ebb and flow of corporate performance practically guarantees seasons. There are seasons the company needs to focus on cash generation and seasons where it can invest money in strategic opportunities. It's important to assess where you are as a firm and to use that as a basis for prioritization. In Figure 5.1, we can see how this may play out.

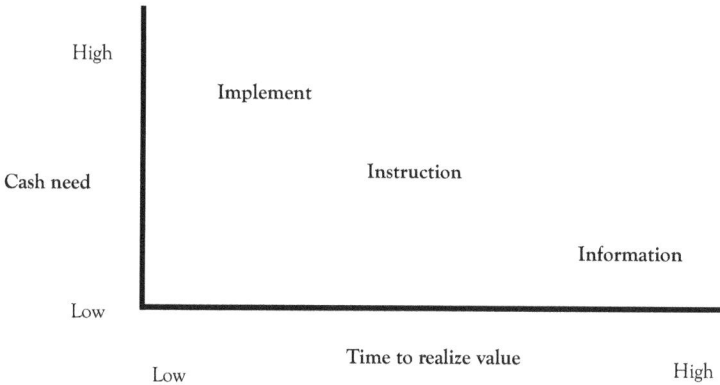

Figure 5.1 By mapping the time to realize value and the need for cash, companies can get guidance regarding the type of project they should look to implement

Companies in need of quick cash may give Implement projects the highest priority because they may be the fastest path to cash. Second would be Instruction because it creates a plan that positions the company to be one step away from a project that can be fully implemented. The lowest priority may be Insight, where there is a much further lapse between when the recommendations are made, and the program creates cash value.

The opposite of this is the scenario where the company is in a good cash position and can look to make investments in the future. This situation, from my experience, is seen more frequently with private companies where there is little to no pressure from shorter term investors. Private owners may be in a position to make decisions for the future by taking a step back, asking questions, and seeking solutions to opportunities that will lay the groundwork for future performance.

The third scenario is when a company should act to improve its cash position in the medium term. In that context, focusing on laying out plans will set up future opportunities that can, too, lead to implementation when the timing is right. It is almost a lock and load scenario where, when the company is ready to move, it has project opportunities identified and justified, and all that is left is to pull the trigger and implement the chosen opportunities.

Once the company scenario is established and agreed upon, the suggestion is that the leadership should stick to that as a basis for comparison for a period of time. The reason is, if you change too frequently, the prioritization scheme, too, will change, leaving the company in a position where decisions become challenging because the basis for making the decision and the criteria used are shifting.

Lead Time to Value

The lead time to value factor is one that should strongly be considered when selecting projects. The amount of time to implement a project may be enough of an impetus to choose an Instruction project over an Implement project. For example, as mentioned in Chapter 2, I was once a part of a strategy project where the initial returns were substantial as projected, but the project cash payback was 72 months. This was not acceptable to our customer, so we had to redesign the project so that we could reduce the lead time to value. We subsequently broke down the single project into a series of projects that were basically self-funding.

If it takes 36 months from now to realize the financial value with an Implementation project, but an Instruction project can realize a reasonable amount of value in 18 months, the Instruction project may be the right direction to go with all things being equal and if the company is in a position where it needs cash.

One factor to consider in situations like this is to provide, when possible, a pathway to value for the Informational and Instructional opportunities. This pathway includes the value opportunity, the time and effort to realize value, and the potential risks. A savvy manager knows precision isn't an option at this stage and that the actual value projection, alone, will not be extraordinarily useful due to the numerous uncertainties that exist between identifying a potential opportunity, establishing the plan, and actually executing the plan. In cases like this, I've actually found it more valuable to come up with a best- and worst-case scenario to create boundaries for the estimate. With each, you document the assumptions that determine the upper and lower limits of what is possible. We can then discuss the assumptions to assess the plausibility, and to create a level of trust in the projections.

Size of the Opportunity

Finally, opportunity size and type should be important considerations as well. In general, projects with the greatest returns should be given priority, again, all things being equal. The key, however, is in the proper documentation and consideration of cash value. As mentioned in Chapter 2, and as we will see in the next two chapters, project value can be inflated when noncash costs, $cost_{NC}$, are added to cash costs, $cost_C$, creating a large number with currency as its unit of measure as we saw with Oracle. There is a way to keep this from happening.

One recommendation is to articulate capacity and cash improvements separately. We will find, creating BCC Models with capacity maps, that most improvement projects begin by improving capacity use. Capacity improvement refers to the amount of capacity saved or that will not be used as a result of the improvement. For instance, increasing efficiency leads to either less capacity consumed to create output, or for the same consumption of capacity, one can create more output. As an example, improvements may either allow someone to perform 10 tasks in 30 versus 60 minutes, or they can now perform 20 tasks versus 10 tasks in the same time. It is the improvement in capacity use that, in most cases, enables steps that lead to cash savings.

Cash improvement will be tied to the rate of $cash_{IN}$ and $cash_{OUT}$, which are affected by how much capacity is purchased and how much output is sold and paid for. One does not directly lead to the other. In the example above, doing things more efficiently doesn't mean the company is spending less on capacity. Hence, there is an improvement to capacity use but not to $cash_{OUT}$. This will help leaders understand where the improvement was made, whether there was a direct cash impact, and if not, what options exist to improve cash as a result of the improvements in capacity use.

As discussed later in the book, documenting capacity savings first is the preferred method. The numbers or values we use to calculate capacity and cash improvements, of course, are raw, unprocessed data, meaning there are no accounting dollar values tied to the opportunity. If we lease 7,500 square feet, for example, and 1,500 square feet is organized for use, we can see we now have an additional 20 percent of space available for use. If we have 5,000 square feet being used for offices, and our space utilization went from 86.7 percent down to 67 percent, we know that one-third or 1,700 square feet will be available for other use. Compare this to suggesting you've saved $2,375 in capacity costs. What does that mean from practical or managerial perspectives? Additionally, it's a $cost_{NC}$ value anyway, so it's of no cash value. Your lease will not go down because you use space more efficiently. Of course, without knowing where the number came from, you can't back into how much actual capacity you can now use for something else. The average person would not be able to convert the $2,375 into how much space was saved, or how much is available for use without a good amount of context. The capacity-based approach also allows for relative improvement sizes to be compared easily across projects with no ambiguity and no false financial savings.

When considering the cash savings and the size of the opportunity, we have to think about how the improvement will affect $cash_{IN}$ and $cash_{OUT}$. The next two chapters will explain in much more detail how we do this, but the cash calculation and the requisite management actions necessary to achieve the cash benefits should be the determining factors regarding how large the cash opportunity truly is.

Some will still find the need to put a dollar value on capacity savings. This is highly discouraged, but if required, the suggestion is A. The technique for calculating value should remain consistent and, B. The value is not combined with cash savings to create a total dollar savings. The values are different, as one is cash and the other is not. Hence, adding them together makes no mathematical sense and can compromise managerial decision making.

Next chapter, we will discuss how improvement projects create value for organizations.

Key Takeaways

1. When considering improvement projects, strategic alignment is important. Each project should be assessed on its salience.

2. The type of project, too, is important. Informational and Instructional projects will not lead to cash value on their own. This does not mean they are not important. It just means if the company seeks cash returns, the only way to achieve them is through Implementation projects.

3. Companies should have a standard way to prioritize projects. The recommendation here is to do so by using the Project Prioritization Matrix, which both aligns the improvement opportunity with the company's strategy and considers the cash generation potential of the opportunity.

4. The Project Prioritization Matrix should be a first step and not an end-all, be-all for decision making. Other factors such as the time to value, and opportunity potential should be considered.

CHAPTER 6

The Source of Value

Generally, improvement projects by themselves do not lead to cash value improvement. They enable cash value improvement by changing how efficiently and effectively we use capacity. As such, it's important to understand what the limitations of improvement projects are, and what steps managers must take to ensure cash value improvement.

To this point in the book, I've talked a lot about this notion of cash value. One important question is, "What is cash value?" This chapter will delve into answering this question by creating a contextual definition of value, discussing where value comes from in the context of improvement projects, and then discussing the path to cash value via capacity improvements. I will do this by focusing on answering the following questions:

- What is value?
- What are the types of value?
- How do improvement projects create value? and
- How do we manage cash value realization?

What Is Value?

We often hear people using the term *value* freely and ambiguously. The question is, "What is value?" I believe it is important that we define the term so that we can eliminate as much ambiguity as possible. This will put us all on the same page and allow us to understand and work toward common goals.

Value, here, is defined simply as the positive effect created by the improvement project. More specifically, think about answering the following questions:

"What will be better as a result of implementing this project?"

"Why will it be better?"; and

"To what extent?"

These elements will help us understand, define, and document how the project will improve the business. Additionally, since this book is focused on cash generation, we will understand whether the improvement itself can lead to cash improvement, and if not, help us define the steps that are necessary to achieve the cash value. This process begins with documenting the direct value the improvement project has.

Documenting Value

For us to see the impact or anticipated impact from the project, we have to document the changes that are directly created by the project. If we go back to Chapter 4, the Operations and Cash, or OC Domain was central to modeling operations, cash, capacity, and business activity. Recall, also, the four key business activities of the BCC Model buy, consume, create, and sell.

Capacity maps, as discussed in Chapter 4, are an effective tool for modeling the OC Domain and the associated business activities. As mentioned previously, capacity maps help us understand how much capacity we've bought and what the cash implication is, how much we've consumed, how much output was created, and of that, how much was sold (Figure 6.1). For example, looking at Figure 6.2, we see if we pay $30 per hour for the capacity, we know we bought eight hours for $240. We know we consumed seven of the eight hours or 87.5 percent of the capacity we bought and created 56 units of output for an average of eight units per productive hour or seven units per purchased hour. Adding sales, assuming we sell 50 of them for six dollars each, we would generate $300 in revenue this period assuming all sales are recovered in the current period (Figure 6.3). Hence, we have generated $300 and spent $240 for the period suggesting we made $60 cash. We know this without calculating

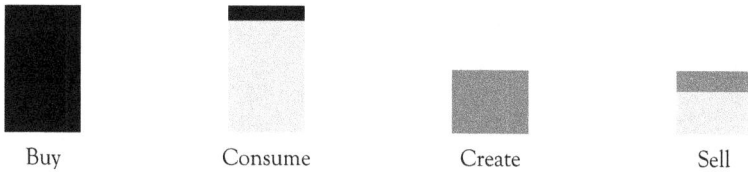

Figure 6.1 Capacity maps represent how business is transacted, from buying capacity, through consuming that capacity to create output. When the output is salable, it compares how much output was created to the demand for the output. From capacity maps comes a wealth of information on cash, business activity, and business efficiency, effectiveness, and efficacy

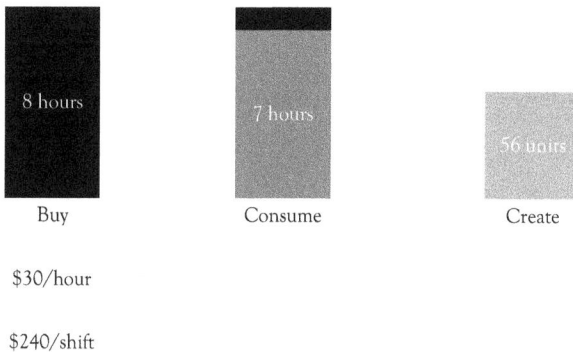

$30/hour

$240/shift

Figure 6.2 This is a traditional capacity map without sales being shown. It describes how much capacity we bought, what we paid for it, how much of the capacity was consumed, and how much output was created from the consumed capacity

a single unit cost. We can also see we produced in excess of demand suggesting we were overproductive.

For the purposes of this book, and as suggested generally when using the Business Domain Management framework, we will focus on modeling business and cash activities in the OC Domain using capacity maps.[1] This is where the business activity happens and will be the target for improvement

---

[1] Lee 2018.

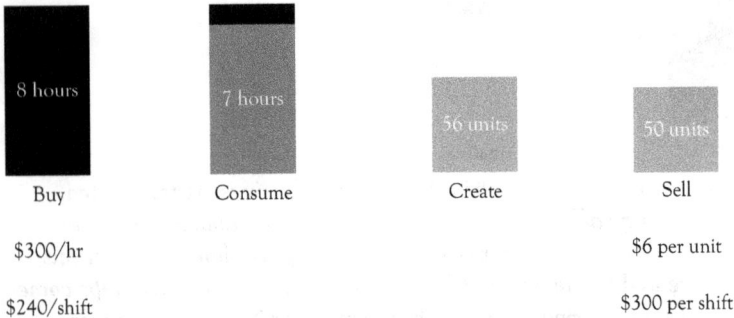

| Buy | Consume | Create | Sell |
| 8 hours | 7 hours | 56 units | 50 units |

$300/hr $6 per unit

$240/shift $300 per shift

Figure 6.3 Here, we have a capacity map that considers both sales and demand. Demand for output, whether salable or not, should set the context for how much capacity we need and to buy, how we consume it, and how much output it should create. For instance, in this case, we see that we created more output than was necessary, suggesting we could potentially meet demand with less capacity. Notice we did not have this context in Figure 6.2

projects. It is where we make decisions regarding how much capacity we need, when we buy it, how much we buy, and how we will use it. This affects $cash_{OUT}$. It's also where we make the decisions regarding output levels, which influences our efficiency, effectiveness, and productivity. Finally, it's where we actually create output, whether for external or market purchase and consumption, or used internally by coworkers. This helps us understand the demand for capacity. When we understand capacity and capacity consumption rates, we can start with demand, determine how much capacity is necessary to meet that demand at both current and post improvement rates, and then back into the amount of capacity we need to buy, which is critical when managing $cash_{OUT}$.

When output is salable, it *may* help our $cash_{IN}$. In Figure 6.3, we can see that we exceeded demand, so although there were more items to sell, if there is no demand, there are no sales. This challenges the notion that generally increasing output will lead to sales. This is not true as discussed in Chapter 2.

These elements of the business are exactly what improvement projects focus on, and where they will subsequently create value. For instance, in Figure 6.4, we can see that we have created value by reducing the amount of input necessary to create the same level of output. By documenting how we do business initially and how things would be in the future as a result of the improvement project using capacity maps, we should see discernible differences between the two.

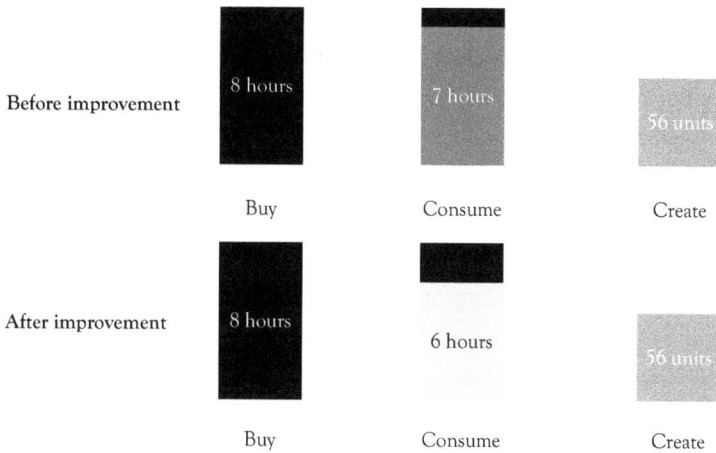

Figure 6.4 This capacity map shows how many techniques create value. By requiring less capacity to create output, companies now have additional capacity that can either be filled with value adding work or eliminated if not needed. Because the amount of capacity we buy has not changed in this case, the improvement will not affect cash$_{OUT}$

Types of Value

There are two types of value that improvement projects create and that we will focus on. The first is the operational value described previously. This is the improvement to operations that can or will result from implementing the project. The second is the marginal improvement in cash resulting from or enabled by the project.

The path to cash value (Figure 6.5) will begin by creating operational value. How will operations be improved as a result of our project, as shown with capacity maps. However, this is not enough. The reason is, improvement projects improve our efficiency in the context of creating output. As we will

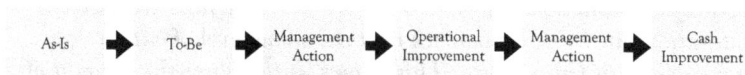

Figure 6.5 The path to value realization involves improving the current state (As-Is) to a future state (To-Be). The To-Be state should enable an improvement to the As-Is state. However, the changes do not usually happen automatically. Oftentimes, managerial action will be required to achieve the operational value

see later in the chapter, cash is spent on what we buy, so even if we can create more output or take less capacity to create output, if the amount we buy does not change, there will be no cash savings. In many cases, additional managerial steps must be executed to achieve the cash value. For instance, looking at Figure 6.4, we can see that the same amount of money was spent before the improvement as we spent after the improvement.

Likewise, with sales limited to 50 units in the example, revenue will be capped at $300. The improvement had no cash benefit as demonstrated by the capacity map. Only when we make changes will we see changes in cash. If we take managerial steps, we can realize cash savings as demonstrated shown in Figure 6.6. Initially, we since we can create the same output with less input, we can buy less input and still be as productive.

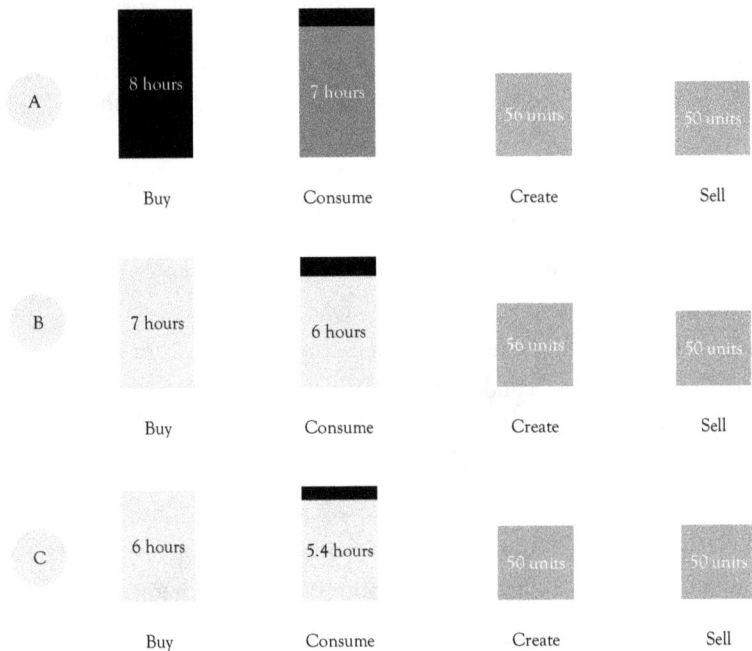

Figure 6.6 The operational value in this case is tied to reducing capacity consumption from 7 to 6 hours. In A, we have the current state situation. In B, we can see that the same level of output can be created with fewer hours. This allows us to reduce the amount of capacity purchased (from 8 to 7, reducing cash$_{OUT}$ by $30. In C, by aligning output, we reduce the amount of capacity necessary to meet demand. This allows for a further reduction in capacity of one hour. Notice, however, that capacity costs are only saved when management buys less capacity

If we look to align output with demand, we will find an even greater opportunity to reduce cash$_{OUT}$. We can actually meet demand by buying six hours of capacity rather than eight, saving \$60 in the process. This doesn't happen automatically, however. Someone must purposefully change how much capacity is purchased for the cash savings to be realized. Repurposing people is positive from a human resources perspective, but it will have no effect on cash$_{OUT}$. There will be more on this in Chapter 7.

How Do Improvement Projects Create Value?

To understand how improvement projects create value, we need to first consider what will be improved. Let's begin by taking a deeper dive into capacity. We buy capacity in the form of labor, space, materials, equipment, and technology. When we buy this capacity, the following is usually the case; we pay an amount for a fixed amount of capacity and the cash cost does not change with use. For instance, what we pay for 5,000 square feet does not change with how we use it, just like your salary does not change with the work that you do. Likewise, what we pay for materials doesn't change when we consume it. It only changes with what we buy. This type of capacity is called static or input capacity. It is static because we buy a fixed amount. It is input because it's what we will start with to create output. Without this capacity, we would not be able to create output. We would need to rely on another source.

The second type of capacity is dynamic or output capacity. Output capacity is what we can create with the input capacity. Offices and storage space as outputs are made available from the space input we bought. Widgets as output are created from the labor, material, and equipment capacity we bought. Projects, as output, are created, executed, and delivered from the labor capacity we bought.

Because output can vary, it is dynamic and referred to as dynamic capacity.[2] Two people may, based on differing skill sets, have different output levels when doing the same work over the same period. The same person will have varying output levels for the same amount of time at different moments. For instance, our productivity in the morning for one hour may be different from our productivity during an hour in the afternoon.

---

[2] Ibid, 58.

There is a theoretical maximum output level and the actual realized output level.[3] Both play a role in capacity planning and management. Theoretical helps us understand what is truly possible while the actual helps us understand what we achieved. The two do not need to be the same. In fact, as we will see later in the chapter, the actual should be tied to creating an efficient, effective, and productive way to meet demand when looking to focus on cash. We will see that accounting information may sometimes drive us, unnecessarily, toward aligning them, which may suboptimize overall performance.

Improvement projects create operational value by increasing efficiency. Efficiency is defined as the ratio of output to input (Equation 6.1).

$$\text{Efficiency } (\in) = \text{output} \div \text{input} \qquad \text{(Eq. 6.1)}$$

Efficiency as an expression of capacity is found in Equation 6.2.

$$\in = \text{output capacity} \div \text{input capacity} \qquad \text{(Eq. 6.2)}$$

We are familiar with this relationship. Consider fuel efficiency. We buy one gallon of gas (input), and we drive (output). Assuming we go 20 miles and use the entire gallon of gas, we will say that our fuel efficiency is 20 miles per gallon. Now assume either improvements in driving style, conditions, or improvements to the vehicle now allow you to drive 25 miles on a gallon of gas. You have increased your fuel efficiency from 20 miles per gallon to 25 miles per gallon (Figure 6.7). With this improvement, you can either drive farther with the same input, or go the same distance with less input.

The same holds true with our work. Assume there are 10 customer service issues to be addressed by 5 customer service reps. If we can automate the process so that only four reps are required, we have increased our efficiency.

Improvement projects generally target efficiency improvements in general, and improvements to consumption, and output rates specifically. When you consider the benefits of IT, for example, you may get data and information faster, it may be of higher quality, or its value to you is now much greater. You can get the same work done in less time. These examples are like driving 20 miles using less gas. When you reach

---

[3] R.T. Yu-Lee. 2003. "Don't Miss the Bottom Line with Productivity." *Increases Industrial Management*, 8–13.

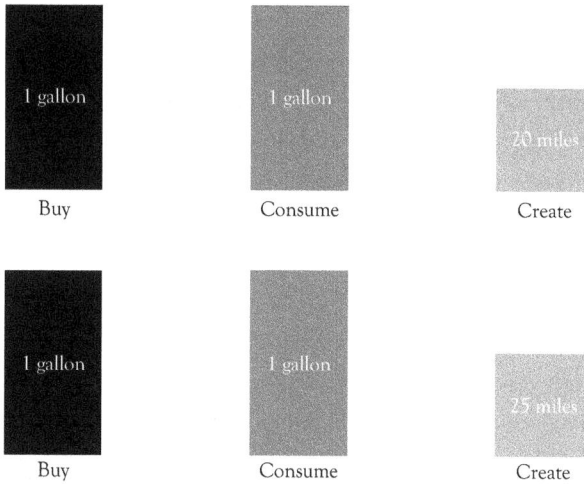

Figure 6.7 *This capacity map shows creating more output with the same input increases efficiency. For the same investment in input, we can get greater output. This is one example of an efficiency increase. Another example comes from considering there is less capacity required to meet demand. For example, if you only need to go 20 miles, you no longer need a full gallon of gas. You only need 8/10 of a gallon of gas. Hence, you can create the same output using less input*

the desired destination, you'd have more input capacity, gas, than you normally would. You can get to your desired output level using less capacity because your IT solution has simplified tasks, for example. The other side of IT improvements is that they may allow you to get more accomplished in the same amount of time. This is akin to being able to drive farther with one gallon. In the same period, you can process more invoices or sign off on more documents.

In the end, you are more efficient, but that you are more efficient doesn't mean your company is paying less for capacity. They are not paying you less. They're paying you the same, so cash$_{OUT}$ remains exactly the same and in this context, forgetting about the investment to realize the improvement, the cash level stays the same. This is where I encounter resistance from naysayers discussing what else they believe the improvements enable:

"Oh, but we can sell more!" Most output in organizations is not salable, and for that which is, we are assuming there is demand for the output. If not, there is not more sales.

"Oh, but my cost per unit has gone down!" How does an ill-conceived number that decreases when cash stays the same have any meaningful managerial value (Figure 6.8)?

"We can deploy the people elsewhere, have them do other work!" Yes, you can, but as long as cash$_{OUT}$ is the same, no money has been saved.

What we see is that to reduce cash costs, cost$_C$, we must change input capacity. We either buy less or we buy cheaper. Improvements can only affect output capacity. Input capacity changes with managerial decisions that are enabled by, not because of, the improvements. Improvement projects don't cause changes in how much input capacity is purchased as much as gravity doesn't cause plane crashes. Something must change that enables other factors to take over.

Going back to Figure 6.6, the improvements enabled managers to choose whether they reduced capacity to save on cash$_{OUT}$. They can choose to continue to buy eight hours for no savings, or they can buy seven or six, but these are managerial decisions that must be made and executed.

How Do We Manage Cash Value Realization?

Efficiency brings us operation value. However, we are seeking cash value which, I hope I've demonstrated, doesn't come directly from efficiency improvements. We need the appropriate management actions to convert

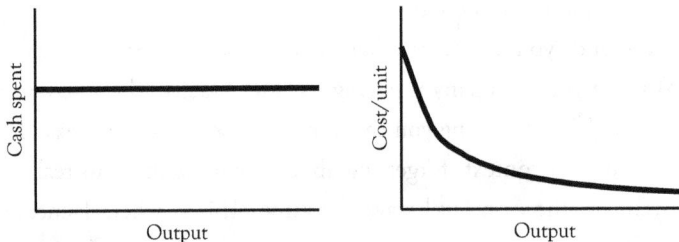

Figure 6.8 When the amount of cash remains the same, there have been no cash benefits. Cost per unit is an Accounting Domain metric that creates an illusion that costs are decreasing. Can you name one scenario where you spend less money making 20 of something than you would making just two?

the operational value to cash value. This happens when we execute decisions that affect cash$_{IN}$ and cash$_{OUT}$. This is *very* important. Managers who do not understand the nature and impact of the improvement and, therefore, what actions they should take can have a neutral value on cash at best and negative value at worst.

Consider the following example of how managers can be bamboozled by an inappropriate understanding of, or approaches to improving cash. In Figure 6.9, we have three step or three operation process to create salable output. The maximum output of this process is five units per hour as constrained by Operation 2. A consultant comes along and demonstrates how Operation 1's efficiency can be increased by 20 percent from 10 units per hour to 12 units per hour (Figure 6.10). Generally, this would create an accounting cost savings but as we can see from the capacity map in Figure 6.11, there has been no change in cash.

What we have here can be easily explained using what I call an isocash curve. As a prefix, *iso* means same or equal. Isocash, therefore, means same

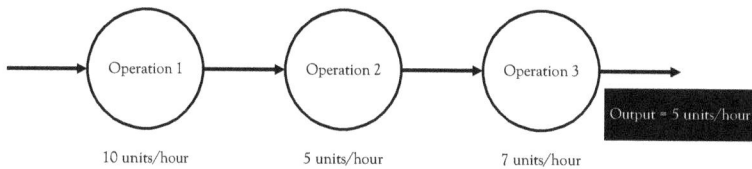

Figure 6.9 A simple three-step process helps us understand the impact of constraints on processes

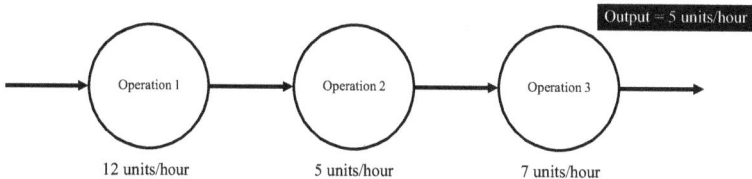

Figure 6.10 Notice that we have increased the output rate of Operation 1, but the output rate of the process has not changed. This means both the output and the revenue (assuming there is demand, that is ≥ 5 units per hour) are constrained by Operation 2. Improving A will have no direct positive cash improvement, and considering the company may have paid for the improvement and the excess materials to take advantage of the increase, there may be a negative cash impact

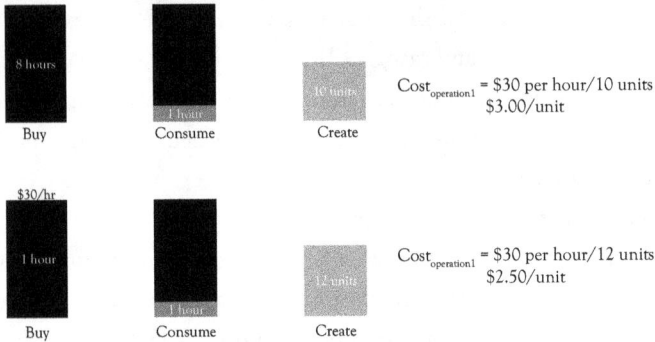

$$Cost_{operation1} = \$30 \text{ per hour}/10 \text{ units}$$
$$\$3.00/\text{unit}$$

$$Cost_{operation1} = \$30 \text{ per hour}/12 \text{ units}$$
$$\$2.50/\text{unit}$$

Figure 6.11 This is a capacity map for Operation 1. As we can see, nothing changes from a cash$_{OUT}$ perspective in the OC Domain even though we can calculate a cost savings for the improvement in the Accounting Domain

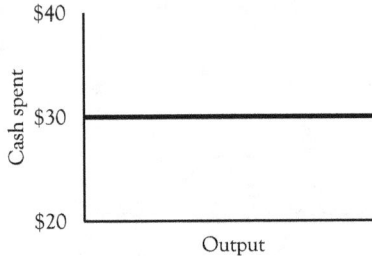

Figure 6.12 The $30 spent for an hour of Operation 1 and the output created are independent of one another

or equal cash. What we pay the person for the shift in this case is $30 per hour as shown in Figure 6.12.

This curve, as we have seen several times before, shows the relationship between what we paid for the capacity and the output created by it. They are, of course, independent. However, when we tried to transform OC Domain data into accounting information, something strange happens. In Figure 6.13, what we see is an isocash curve for one hour of the person's time. In that one hour, we see that as we increase output, we get the impression that unit costs are going down. In this example, we pay the person $30 per hour. If we divide this by units of output, we have one way to calculate a unit cost. Initially, we spent $30 and created 10 units for a cost of three dollars per unit. By increasing the output to 12, we see the cost is reduced to $2.50. From this curve, we see that as we create more output, the cost per unit goes down. However, this is cost$_{NC}$.

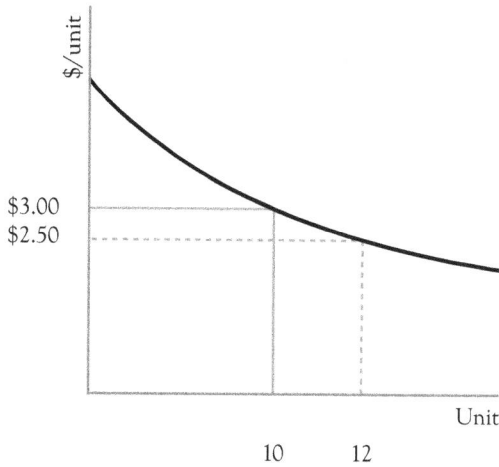

Figure 6.13 This is a typical isocash curve. It is isocash because the curve represents one value of cash. In this case, the cash represents the $30 for an hour of labor. Cost per unit can be calculated from the curve as we see in this case. The curve shows that the cost per unit goes down with increased output although cash spent remains the same

This leads to an extremely important conclusion. Most people in their right mind may consider improving Operation 1 and lowering its unit cost to be a positive. However, the $cash_{OUT}$ is the same or higher. Assume we spent money on the solution. Our $cash_{OUT}$ has increased due to the services purchased and received. To get full *value* from the improvement, one may want maximum use of the capacity. The more products created, the lower the accounting cost. So, the company increases its material consumption rate and therefore the rate of buying material capacity. Seeking efficiency in this case may lead to higher input costs to achieve the artificial $0.50 savings per unit. Additionally, assuming no increase in sales but recognizing the unit cost reduction, selling the product at a higher gross margin can lead to a higher tax base. Given the revenue is five dollars for an initial margin of two dollars versus $2.50 after the improvement, with a higher gross margin, we are increasing our taxable income, which increases $cash_{OUT}$.

This analysis does two things. First, it demonstrates what happens when people focus on accounting value rather than cash value. Decisions can be made in the name of reducing costs or improving profit that have no, or a negative effect on cash. Second, it will discourage actions and decisions that appear positive financially but can be to the company's detriment. Here are a few examples of both.

I once visited a company that made corrugated paper products. During the plant tour, the plant manager bragged about a huge piece of equipment called a corrugator. He mentioned how expensive it was to buy, and to "pay back" the machine, they needed to run it all the time. The facility was in a small town, and the plant manager mentioned that the machine supported the local economy. Why was it felt that the corrugator must be running all the time to "pay for itself" and to "reduce costs?"

Keeping the corrugator running 24/7, for instance, required a lot of labor, material, equipment and space capacity to feed it, run it, unload it, and to store the final product. Later in the tour, we visited the finished goods area where there was inventory everywhere and most had no customer orders tied to it.

One must ask how running a machine and building inventory that is not sold saves money. How does it "pay back" the machine? If more labor and materials are purchased, $cash_{OUT}$ is increasing, yet with finished goods sitting in inventory, there is not a subsequent increase in sales, suggesting that the company is worse off financially not better. So why does this happen?

The primary reason there is focus on efficiency is because of how the improvements are handled in the Accounting Domain. We believe that by increasing efficiency, our costs go down as demonstrated in the isocash curve in Figure 6.13. Recall the two ways of increasing efficiency. The first is to create more output with the same input. The second is to reduce the amount of capacity consumed to create current levels of output as seen in the isocash curve shown in Figure 6.14. In both cases, we see a reduction in the Accounting Domain metric of cost per unit without a subsequent change to $cash_{OUT}$. This causes many to believe they are improving the situation financially when, in fact, they are doing little at best, and damage at worst. By running the corrugator 24/7, the plant manager was extending the "payback" not shortening it, and spending money, not making it.

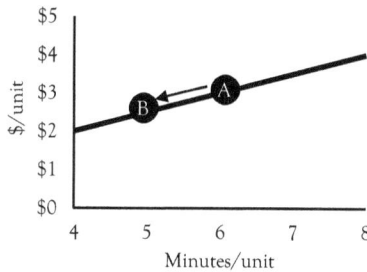

Figure 6.14 This is an example of an isocash curve that considers consumption rates versus output. It represents reductions in cost per unit related to reductions in consumption rates

The second scenario was one I experienced as a professor. In a course designed for graduating seniors, the professor created a problem that compared having an older piece of equipment to a newer piece of equipment and asked the students to compare the scenarios as somewhat of an improvement project. The professor mentioned the salvage value of the older equipment, the price of the newer equipment, improvements in output rates, depreciation rates, and so on. Many of us have performed these analyses.

Nowhere did the professor mention whether the machine was going to improve a nonconstraint such as Operation 1 or whether it was going to be applied to a constraint such as Operation 2, which would improve process output. When performing the financial analysis as set up by the professor, the company in question might spend $40 million on a piece of equipment that would potentially have no effect on $cash_{IN}$. There would be, however, a significant increase in $cash_{OUT}$, which could leave the company in a much poorer position.

Managers are still learning these techniques in universities and by others in their companies, and it leads to poorer, not better, cash performance from improvement projects. If we want improvements to cash, we must model cash and make decisions that affect $cash_{IN}$ and $cash_{OUT}$. Focusing on Accounting Domain information rather than OC Domain cash data will practically guarantee that managerial decision making will suboptimize and, in some cases, sabotage cash value.

Next chapter, we will focus on how to design improvements that do focus on cash and lead us toward the cash improvement we seek.

Key Takeaways

1. Value is the improvement that projects bring to an organization.
2. Most improvements create operational value. Most need managerial action to achieve both operational and financial value.
3. To help managers ensure they understand the operational and cash value opportunities, avoid using Accounting Domain information and, instead, focus on OC Domain data.
4. The key to realizing cash benefits is to model and manage cash and the factors that affect it. When it comes to managerial action, think about the purchase and use of capacity, and the amount of demand it is required to create. Ensure there is alignment between the two.

CHAPTER 7

Design Improvements in the OC Domain

Capacity maps and the BCC Model describe capacity dynamics; how much we have, how it's used, and the output we create with it. Improvement projects will change how we use the capacity or what we can create with it. In limited situations, cash improvements will occur, such as when more output leads directly to more sales. However, in most cases, managers will be required to make changes to realize cash benefits. Capacity maps, used to model the OC Domain, will help us define the impact of our improvement projects, and determine the subsequent steps managers must take to realize cash benefits.

Chapter 6 focused on the source of operational and cash value; how improvement projects improve the use of capacity. Chapter 8 focuses on the financial benefits of improvement projects. This chapter focuses on how to describe the extent to which the project may affect how you operate and will show you how to define the management actions that will be required to achieve cash value. There is a temptation to discuss improvement strategies such as what to do in an expanding, declining, or steady market here. For example, if the market is expanding or declining, what should the capacity strategy be? However, this book focuses on the techniques of documenting and managing the improvement, rather than which tactics or strategies a company should employ.

The documentation happens in four steps:

1. Document current state using As-Is capacity maps.
2. Create improved state using Working capacity maps.
3. Define future state To-Be capacity maps.
4. Describe management action path from As-Is capacity maps to To-Be capacity maps.

From these four steps, we will have a clear picture of how the OC Domain will be transformed by the improvement, and what specific managerial actions will be needed to make the improvement. Let's go through each step.

As-Is Capacity Maps

When documenting the current state, we want to create capacity maps of the process or process steps we want to improve. We begin with the BCC Model by mapping how much capacity we've purchased in its consumption units. For instance, if we buy time, we want to document the amount of input capacity we purchased in time units such as hours, shifts, days, weeks, or months. If we buy space, we document in square feet or square meters. Documenting input capacity in this way allows us to compare the amount of capacity purchased to the amount consumed when creating output.

The next step is to determine the approximate average consumption rates. The last part of the sentence was very carefully worded. There is a desire to want to focus on doing detailed analyses to determine precise consumption rates. It may be tempting to focus on time studies or time sheets to determine these values. My experience suggests this is, at a minimum, overkill and maximally, disruptive and questionably unproductive. Consumption rates for the same task will vary and, at times, significantly. Sometimes the variation is due to a definable cause and sometimes because of natural variation; some days are better than others for an individual, and some people are more efficient than others. To gather precision here may put you in a position of diminishing returns. Does it matter in the OC Domain if you determine a space consumption rate of 5,026 square feet or is approximately 5,000 good enough? The rate of 5,000 as an approximation is fairly easy to come by without hiring a company or assigning tasks to workers who have other things to do, thereby increasing their consumption rates, too. This is especially true when we will be rounding cost and benefit estimates.

Timesheets are even worse. It is common knowledge that practically everyone has at one time or another, put false information on their timesheets. My friend Ed Kless is known to ask rooms filled with professionals if there is anyone who has never put false information on a timesheet. To my knowledge, he has not found a single individual who has never fudged data on a timesheet, and there are a lot of data points because Ed is a very highly sought-after speaker. Sometimes we do not remember how long a task took. Other times, meeting expectations, such as time spent on a task, may cause someone to be less than truthful. The latter is especially true when folks are managing the "cost" of a project. If a task is estimated and therefore budgeted to take two hours and it takes three, there are times where there is pressure to report two rather than three to help manage the "cost" and "profitability" of the project.

We are all estimating; some of the estimation has good intentions ("I honestly believe it took 1.25 hours") to deception ("It was supposed to take one hour, so I will put one hour although it really took 1.25 hours"). When this happens, it consumes capacity to create false numbers, so the questions are, why do it in the first place?, and if we know there are lies, why isn't the information considered highly questionable?

The next step is to determine the output or demand required for the operation or process. Demand is important because when designing our improvements, the idea is to align output with demand. By defining demand here, we can see where we have over- or underproduced. If we overproduced, made more than demand required, it is likely we consumed more capacity than we needed to. To consume it, we must have it, so there is also the chance we spent more on capacity than we needed to, possibly leading to higher $cash_{OUT}$ than necessary. If we underproduced revenue generating items, we may have foregone revenue because we did not have enough output for the market, leading to lower $cash_{IN}$ than is possible. For internal processes and those that are not salable, we're looking at work potentially being delayed or, in some cases, not being completed at all without increasing the capacity available to do the work.

There are two types of demand: essential and extraneous. Essential demand is that which is required by a customer, whether internal or external. It is demand that we use as a basis to determine whether we are being effective in the context of those who require the demand of us. Extraneous demand is any other demand that is not required by a customer. This is not meant to be a judgment or an assessment of demand. However, extraneous demand, when not managed or scrutinized, inflates the

Figure 7.1 When we add extraneous demand to essential demand, we inflate total demand. When we have inflated demand, we tend to justify carrying excess capacity to create output to meet this demand. However, if we reduce extraneous demand, the real demand is lower, which may allow us to meet this demand with less input capacity

perception of the capacity needed (Figure 7.1). When demand is inflated, the perception of the amount of capacity required, too, is inflated, leading to higher than required capacity being purchased.

Once we have documented the demand, we should have a clear picture of the current state and can use this as a foundation for improvement.

Working Capacity Maps

After the current state is documented, we shift to thinking about how the improvement will affect the OC Domain. Something will be different, and our objective is to identify and document the difference, and the extent of the change. This is where Working capacity maps, or Working maps, come in. We will use Working maps in two ways. The first is to document options for how the improvement may change the As-Is scenario. The second is to show the key implementation steps that will take us from As-Is to To-Be. Let's look at both.

Documenting Improvement

As mentioned in Chapter 6, most of the improvements will result from increases in efficiency. Recall, this is either in the form of creating the same or similar output with less input or creating more output from the same level of input. At this stage, we can understand, notionally, what will change. For instance, we may know that we can process invoices faster or handle more service calls than before. However, we need to take it to the next level of precision. Now, what is important is not only what will change, but also the extent to which it will change. If the improvement enables the creation of more dynamic capacity, how much more will it create, how, and how might that affect output and output potential? Recalling the example from Figure 6.6 as Figure 7.2 here, we often find that we have options. A shows the As-Is map. From the improvement, one option might be B, where we choose to buy seven instead of eight hours. Option C, too, is available to us. By showing both options in this case, conversations can occur among leaders and stakeholders to decide just how far they want to go with the improvement. By showing both B and C, implications of both can be considered and based on the considerations, a direction can be chosen.

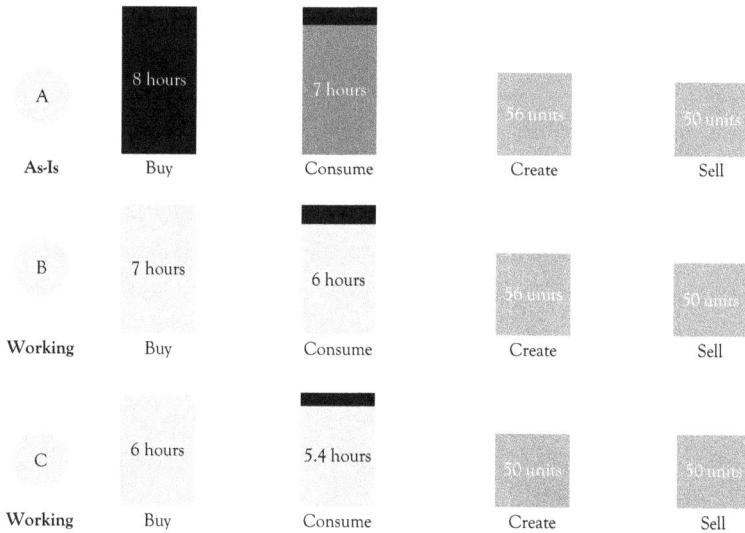

A	8 hours	7 hours	56 units	50 units
As-Is	Buy	Consume	Create	Sell
B	7 hours	6 hours	56 units	50 units
Working	Buy	Consume	Create	Sell
C	6 hours	5.4 hours	50 units	50 units
Working	Buy	Consume	Create	Sell

Figure 7.2 Working capacity maps show us options that are available as a result of improvements. They work well with scenario planning

After the direction is chosen, we have to document the specific managerial actions that need to be taken. For instance, with B, the action is to buy one hour less of input capacity. Looking at this situation, two conclusions should be noted. First, the person is still creating extraneous demand, as the essential demand is for 50 and the output is 56. Management is accepting the notion they are being overproductive in this case. Second, there may be temptation to have the worker do something else with the extra time. That is fine, but since cash$_{OUT}$ is not affected when workers are reassiged, there will be no cash savings.

If C is chosen, the company is taking the extra step to eliminate extraneous demand and is instead, focusing on aligning output with essential demand and reducing input capacity. This will reduce cash$_{OUT}$ for the company because it is buying less labor input and there may be reductions in the amount of material capacity it is buying as well in a products-based environment. This leaves the company with a smaller margin of error, but if they are comfortable with this after the conversations comparing B and C, that is the risk they will take.

Steps Toward To-Be

The other way to use Working maps is to document how and when capacity levels will change as we traverse the path to the To-Be state. Consider a situation where a company may look to lower costs by buying less warehouse space. Initially, the company has 100 thousand square feet of warehouse space, and they are consuming 90 thousand. As a result of the improvement project, they now only need 60 thousand square feet. The company will find and lease 75 thousand square feet at a new location. However, there will be a period where the company will have warehouse capacity at both locations until the move is completed. Once completed, they will move out of the first location and end the lease (Figure 7.3).

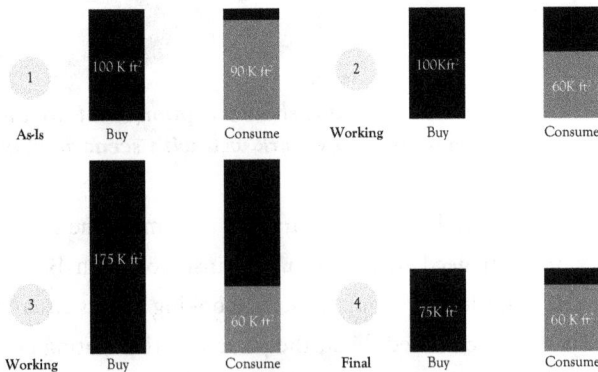

Figure 7.3 Working maps can also describe the progression of improvements that can lead to the desired future state

A Working map used this way does two things. First, it shows the interim steps of the implementation visually. This will help those involved see the steps and understand the changes that are proposed to be made during the implementation. Doing so also demonstrates the team understands the changes that need to be made and the impact they will have on the organization. Second, because the steps are salient, leaders can see that there will be situations where there may be waste during the transition. For example, at step 3, we have a significant amount of extra warehouse capacity. This should create an incentive to move quickly through this step so that the company can minimize cash$_{OUT}$ tied to paying for both warehouses.

To-Be Capacity Maps

The final maps are the To-Be capacity maps. To-Be capacity maps demonstrate the projected future state after the improvement project is completed. Designing the maps involves the same steps as before, however, their use is what is key here. Once determined, To-Be maps should not change until management and the project team agree to do so. They serve as a baseline for improvement and model what the improvement is expected to be. As such, any variances from the To-Be map may affect the benefits expected from implementing the project. For instance, if the organization designed a To-Be map that had 75 thousand square feet of warehouse space but the company ended up with 100 thousand, the reasons this happened and the resulting implications should be documented and discussed. One hundred thousand square feet means they now have an additional 25 thousand square feet. The questions are, why is there a difference? and what is the implication of this difference? Is the lease a lower monthly cost for instance? If someone found a deal and the total cash cost of moving to the 100 thousand square feet location is lower, it might make sense to do so. At that point, the team may agree that the To-Be state will be 100 thousand square feet versus 75 thousand, and the To-Be map and the expected benefits are documented and updated accordingly. Only when there is a change and that change is approved and signed off on, should the To-Be map change.

Management Action

As mentioned in Chapter 6, and earlier in this chapter, improvements, in most cases, are caused by increases in efficiency. They affect efficiency by affecting output or dynamic capacity. Recall, we either make more output consuming the same capacity, or we create the same output by consuming less input capacity. Although the cost per unit of output may have decreased, this is a $cost_{NC}$ reduction. As long as the capacity levels remain the same and unless there is an increase in output that leads directly to sales and not the hope for increased sales, there will be no improvements to cash performance.

The way we get cash benefit is through changing the rate that cash enters and leaves; by changing $cash_{IN}$ and $cash_{OUT}$. Generally, once the improvement is in the implementation phase, changes to $cash_{IN}$ and $cash_{OUT}$ happen through management action. As we've seen, by increasing our efficiency, we position ourselves to have excess input capacity. It is the combination of reducing extraneous demand and making changes to the level of input capacity that will change the input capacity required and, therefore, the amount of input capacity we have to buy. Buying less capacity reduces $cash_{OUT}$. Another option to reduce $cash_{OUT}$ is to buy cheaper capacity.

The process to realize cash benefits from a cost reduction perspective involves looking at the To-Be map and deciding what decisions can lead to reductions in $cash_{OUT}$ with an acceptable level of risk. For instance, we may need to change how much labor or material capacity we buy. In the case of moving space, we may have to spend cash to break a lease before we realize the benefit of cheaper space capacity.

All of the decisions involving changing capacity levels should be identified and documented, both using the Working capacity maps and in the project plan that will be created for the implementation. These are the steps that we will need to take to help us achieve the cash value and that, if we do not execute them, the value potential is reduced. For instance, shifting to a perpetual inventory management system that keeps track of inventory is nice in terms of understanding how much inventory we have. However, if the objective is to reduce inventory, we have to purposefully slow the rate of buying and creating inventory so that demand

and the subsequent consumption can reduce it to the desired levels. This may mean a combination of changes made in procurement, production control or order release, and possibly sales so that demand is greater than production, leading to lower inventory levels. Someone must ensure these changes occur, and that's management.

Sometimes the specifics regarding management activities are difficult to identify because of the uncertainty involved. Uncertainty prohibits us, in many cases, from having a specific improvement projection. For instance, it's often hard to suggest that software that prescreens customer service calls will increase the output of a customer service rep by exactly three calls per hour. When this happens, a technique that works is to bound the potential values. Generally, there is an upper bound that is more optimistic, and a lower bound that is more pessimistic. We establish these bounds to reflect the uncertainty that is involved with implementation. In this example, considering the dynamics of the improvement, we might be able to determine that the improvement may increase the output by between two and five calls. We can lay out the assumptions regarding why it may be two and why it may be five.

We want to describe the situation by asking questions such as what must occur or what must be true to achieve the upper bound. On the lower bound, we ask questions that will paint a clear picture of what may be the cause of us only achieving the lower bound improvement. For instance, considering the upper bound, we may ask, "To achieve five, what must be true?" or "What must we do or what must happen for us to achieve the five?" This will identify the management action that would lead to the upper bound. Similarly, "What conditions must exist for us to only achieve a two call improvement?" or "If these things don't happen, our increase will be limited to just two."

By bounding the opportunity and the associated assumptions and answers to questions, you do two things. First, you reduce doubt that may affect the decision to move forward. For instance, assume you suggest your project improvement will yield a four call improvement. If someone has reservations regarding whether exactly four will be achieved, the improvement may be halted, delayed, or questioned because the value, itself, may be questioned; four or not four becomes the defining criterion. If someone does not believe the improvement may yield a four call improvement, they may hinder the process by arguing the projection is incorrect. When bounding the value opportunity, there's usually not a yes or no question being pondered. Instead, the conversation shifts to where, between the bounds in the improvement opportunity continuum, are we most likely to fall and the extent to which the assumptions can be affected or influenced by management action (Figure 7.4). This is covered in a bit more detail in Chapter 8 as we think about the specifics regarding documenting how much benefit will result from the implementation.

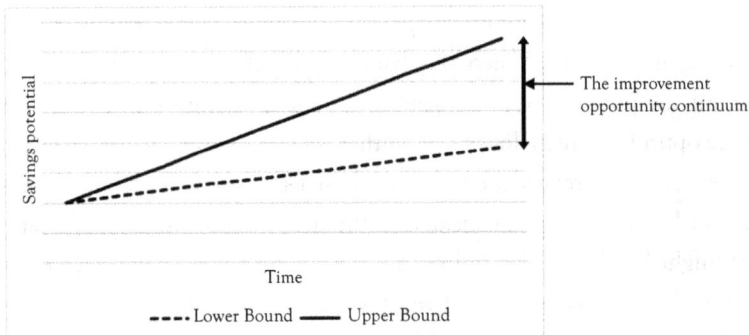

Figure 7.4 The improvement opportunity continuum represents where the team believes the potential value will be. Both the upper and lower bounds should be identified with associated assumptions and management action supporting the bounded values. It's important to have broad conversations about the assumptions and the value with key stakeholders. This will help gain their buy-in and reduce the risk of an aborted or delayed project

Once we have identified the future state, the path to achieving the future state, the managerial actions required, and the range of possibility for the improvements due to uncertainty, we look to determine the financial benefits generated and project those benefits into the future. That is the subject of the next chapter.

Key Takeaways

1. All improvements should be modeled in the OC Domain. The Business Activity Framework serves as the basis for how the business operates, what we are looking to change, and the cash impact of the change. Note, the Accounting Domain has no role in this process.

2. We can model the improvements using capacity maps. As-Is, Working, and To-Be capacity maps show the current state, the future state, and the steps that are involved to traverse the path to improvement.

3. When going from the As-Is map to the To-Be map, there will be management steps required to change components of the Business Activity Framework so that cash improvements will be realized. It is important to begin documenting these activities as we think about what is required to achieve the improvements.

4. It is highly recommended that improvement projections are bounded showing an upper and lower bound. This will help avoid lengthy debates. It will also help the team understand the potential improvement, what assumptions must be addressed, and the management steps necessary to achieve the desired level of performance and to avoid the undesired.

CHAPTER 8

Financial Benefits and Benefit Projection

Management action affecting capacity levels and use will have a significant impact on the financial benefits. Last chapter we modeled the changes using capacity maps. Next we will need to project the timing and amount of cash benefits that will result from the changes.

Thus far in the book, we've focused on getting to the point where we can design our improvements to realize cash value. We started by focusing on what it takes to realize cash benefits. We then looked at the types of improvement projects there are, how they generate value, the steps necessary to document the improvements, and the management action required to realize cash improvements. This chapter is focused on documenting the benefits and projecting them into the future so that we know when to expect cash benefits and how much to expect.

Key to this process will be using the BCC Model and the capacity maps we created in Chapter 7. As we have seen, capacity maps are used to describe the input capacity levels, capacity consumption rates, and output rates. Since this chapter is focused on identifying the financial value of the improvement, capacity maps will show, clearly, where there are and are not cash benefits. This is where people would typically use cost, managerial accounting, or cost accounting information. However, as discussed in Chapters 3 and 4, accounting information is not useful when calculating the cash benefits and profitability of a project. In fact, it can sometimes be harmful.

Recall, cost and managerial accounting create cost values that are not cash. For instance, consider the following scenario discussed in Chapter 6. We started with an As-Is capacity map where we buy an hour of time for $30. The current output level is 10 units. One possible cost would be $3 per unit when using the entire hour as a cost basis (Figure 8.1).

After the improvement, we assumed output increased from 10 to 12 with the same capacity consumption rates (Figure 8.2). There may be a calculated cost reduction of 50 cents as shown in Figure 8.3. However,

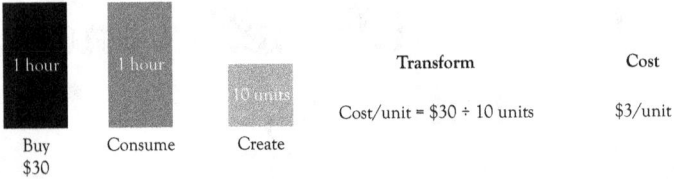

			Transform	Cost
1 hour	1 hour	10 units	Cost/unit = $30 ÷ 10 units	$3/unit
Buy $30	Consume	Create		

Figure 8.1 *Our initial capacity map before improvements are made to output*

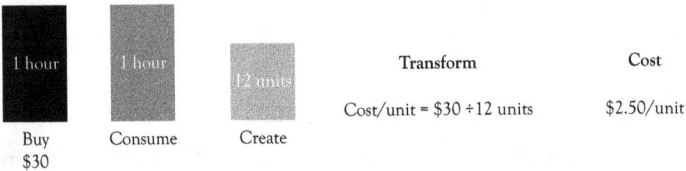

			Transform	Cost
1 hour	1 hour	12 units	Cost/unit = $30 ÷ 12 units	$2.50/unit
Buy $30	Consume	Create		

Figure 8.2 *With an increase in output rate with the same buy–consume attributes, we can calculate a lower unit cost even though the $cash_{OUT}$ has not changed*

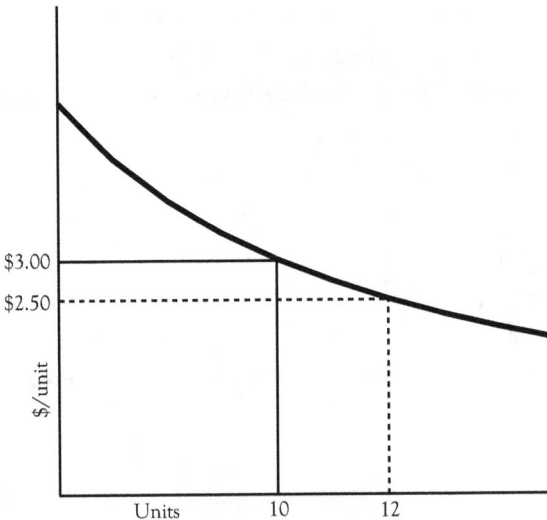

Figure 8.3 *This isocash curve shows why there is no change in $cash_{OUT}$ from the capacity map in Figure 8.2*

we are still on the same isocash curve suggesting nothing has changed from a cash perspective. Hence, the direct cash savings opportunity is zero. The harm comes from assuming these cost savings represent cash and, therefore, are used in the financial justification of the project. They do not represent cash and should not be used to justify projects on a cash basis. This doesn't mean there is no benefit opportunity, as there are noncash opportunities that result from the improved use of capacity. As discussed several times previously, the initial lack of cash savings doesn't mean there is no opportunity for cash improvement. The improved use of capacity may enable managerial decisions, and it's the management action that creates the cash improvement. It is here where we should focus our cash value creation efforts. When calculating the improvements in cash, we want to focus specifically on factors that affect $cash_{IN}$ and $cash_{OUT}$, as these are the only factors that affect cash (Figure 7.5). Let's discuss both.

$Cash_{IN}$

The focus with $cash_{IN}$ is documenting the extent to which there will be an improvement in the rate and timing of cash coming into the organization. There can be a significant difference between the two, so understanding this difference is key. In one case, the issue is about creating a marginal increase in $cash_{IN}$, such as when there is an increase in sales. From increased sales, $cash_{IN}$ may increase from $1,000 per day, for instance, to $1,200, and this increase is solely from increasing the daily sales rate. The other situation is about timing of accounts receivable. If sales are $1,000 per day but day sales outstanding is 45 days, there may be opportunities to collect the cash in fewer days. While improving collections, there may be an increase in daily cash receipts, but that is only collecting what is already due in, so there is no increase in sales. Hence, while there may be increases in cash receipts initially, once outstanding receivables get down to the target levels, the $cash_{IN}$ rate will will be represented by a delay in the rate of sales.

In the first case, the challenge is determining the extent to which revenue will be increased. To increase sales, the improvement project must lead to increased demand and there must be the ability to meet it, either currently or by increasing the output levels. With this, there is a level of uncertainty involved with estimating the increase in sales because demand is often not known with certainty. What is the growth potential? We hope, at a minimum, we will maintain our current sales after the improvement project, but what will the maximum be? If the improvement project increases output potential, how much of the increased output will be absorbed by the market?

In cases like this, as mentioned in the last chapter, we will want to bound the opportunity to help deal with the uncertainty. Ideally, the future sales will not dip below current sales. However, through solution design and bounding the projections, we will need to carefully document what could happen, or not, that may cause a reduction in sales. If there is enough knowledge of an increase in demand, the lower bound may be higher than our current sales. On the high end, there will have to be a guess, and this value is tied to how you handle uncertainty. The higher the uncertainty, the greater the risk, so managing the uncertainty is key to effective projections.

When there is uncertainty, it is tied to that which is unknown (Figure 8.4).[1] All that is initially unknown is not unknowable, however. Market research, for instance, which may range from surveys to asking

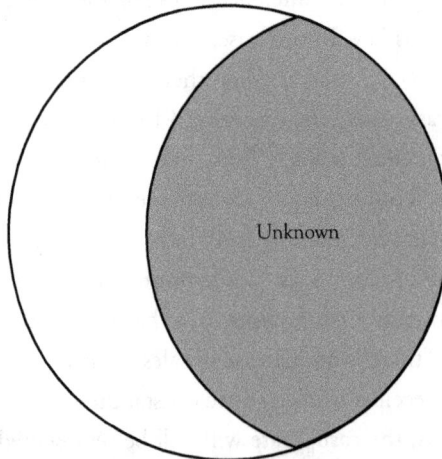

Unknown

Figure 8.4 In the world of information, there is that which is known and that which is unknown

---

[1] H. Courtney. 2001. 20/20 Foresight: Crafting Strategy in an Uncertain World (1st ed.). *Harvard Business School Press.*

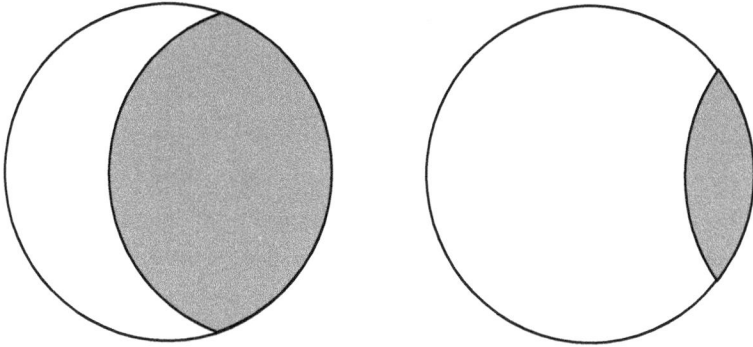

Figure 8.5 How much of that which is currently unknown is truly unknowable? The unknown drives uncertainty and, therefore, risk. If we can reduce that which is unknown but not unknowable, we can reduce uncertainty

for sales commitments, may help you understand some element of the unknown potential demand. The objective is to work to minimize the unknown (Figure 8.5). The upper and lower bounds on the improvement continuum will become closer in value as uncertainty is reduced.

The keys to improving cash through increasing sales are, (1) State the assumptions for the boundaries by asking what must be true for the optimistic projections to be realized, and what must go wrong for the pessimistic assumptions to come true so we understand what is required to achieve the benefits we seek, and (2) manage overactivity in the name of being overly optimistic. Overactivity in this context means buying more than is necessary or creating more than is necessary. There is a risk to optimism, as it can lead to a negative impact on cash when wrong. Oftentimes, extra capacity is purchased in anticipation of creating excess salable output. The money is spent, the output is created, and the sales do not come as anticipated or desired.

The capacity impact of overproduction is often hidden by the numbers in the Accounting Domain. For instance, excess inventory is put on the balance sheet, and as a result, the impact of the decision, from a cash perspective, is difficult to see. Can you see the cash impact of overtime, used to create excess output, on the next payroll cycle clearly by looking at inventory on the balance sheet? The answer is, "no." In fact, the increased output may even lower the product cost, leading to a potential incentive to create more output, all without knowing or realizing the negative impact of the increased cash$_{OUT}$.

In estimating sales increases, in addition to bounding the amount of the increase, we will have to consider the timing. When considering increased output, we will have to think about the particulars regarding how output will be increased, the steps to implement these particulars, and then the expected rate and timing of increase of sales. These are important when determining how long it will take to realize the increased $cash_{IN}$, compared to the expenditures necessary to realize the value.

Regarding the timing of cash receipts, there are a couple factors to consider.

1. What having the cash creates;
2. What having the cash eliminates.

Having the Cash Creates

There are many benefits associated with having cash from reducing receivables, such as less time and, therefore, capacity involved in collecting it, and the ability to invest the capital for longer periods. The key will be to model the improvements and management actions effectively. If there were capacity used collecting cash, how much of that capacity can be freed by reducing the demand on it from the collections activities? What will this enable management to do to affect $cash_{OUT}$? It's quite possible it won't, but the opportunity should be considered. If the capacity is not reduced, $cash_{OUT}$ will not change. Additionally, improved working capital investment requires the cash to actually be invested; sooner rather than later. If you have the cash and do not make it work for you, the ability for it to generate more cash is compromised. We will want to model the $cash_{OUT}$ for the investment and any returns we may anticipate, but only those we anticipate during the analysis period. Clearly, with investments, we are dealing with uncertainty based on the type of investments and the variability/risk involved, so both the benefit and the timing of the return will need to be bounded.

What Having the Cash Eliminates

Having the cash does two things. First, as mentioned previously, there is less of a need to chase the cash, so less capacity will be spent doing so, and resorting to actions such as factoring the receivables, which can lead to a lower cash$_{IN}$ and the potential for an increased cash$_{OUT}$ to cover the costs of factoring can be avoided. A second key concept is that by having the money, hopefully the need for future loans can be reduced. Clearly this reduces the cash impact of borrowing the money.

The keys with cash$_{IN}$ are to be diligent in modeling the improvement, the steps or managerial actions necessary to achieve the benefits, and to state the assumptions when bounding the opportunities. Oftentimes, the optimism is too high and the pessimism is too low because of the pressure to show improvement. It's best that both are tempered, challenged, and the assumptions stated and agreed on so that the projections are believed to be more realistic.

Cash$_{OUT}$

The largest opportunities are generally found by adjusting cash$_{OUT}$. As mentioned several times throughout the book, improvements are enabled by making capacity more efficient. We also learned efficiency improvements keep you on the same isocash curve and, therefore, do not lead to reductions in cash$_{OUT}$. To achieve the benefits in cash$_{OUT}$, you must move to another isocash curve (Figure 8.6). This happens when you change the amount of input capacity you buy or the price you pay for it. These

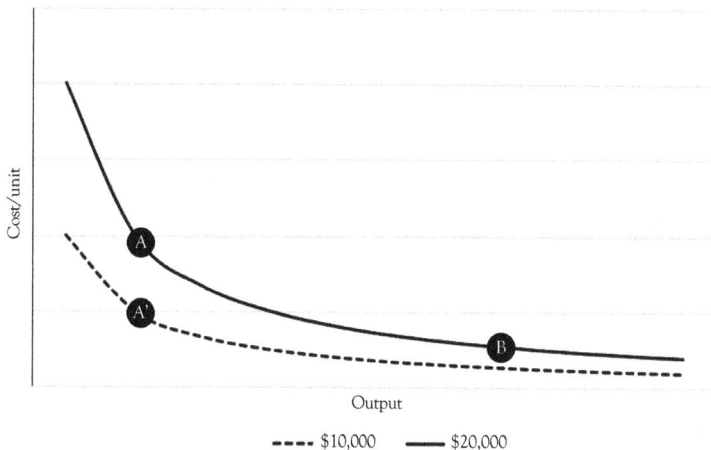

Figure 8.6 Increasing efficiency by going from A to B will lower the unit cost. However, it will not affect cash$_{OUT}$. Moving from A to A' is a shift in isocash curves, repesenting a lower cash$_{OUT}$

changes lead directly to cash improvements. The difference between the input capacity levels on the As-Is capacity map and the To-Be capacity map becomes the source of documenting the cash value opportunity. *How much less capacity at a given price are we buying? How much of the same capacity at a lower price are we buying?* The management action involves the steps necessary to shift operations from the current state to the desired state. This process simply involves documenting the cash value of the capacity reduction created by management action.

As we look to document the cash benefit of the changes, we have to be diligent and precise about what has changed. When we think about capacity reduction numbers, we have to understand how much capacity we are getting rid of, when, and how that will affect cash$_{OUT}$. And the process must be considered comprehensively. For instance, when looking to buy fewer materials, how much less are we going to buy and when? When can be affected by how much inventory we currently have and promises we've made to buy from our vendors. Additionally, if we are going to buy at a lower cost, are there fees associated with getting out of current contracts? At what point can we take advantage of lower prices? Considering the warehouse example from Chapter 7, if we need to break a lease, how big of a price tag is it to get out, when will we pay it, and for what period of time will we have two leases we are paying for while working toward shutting down the older warehouse? If we are reducing labor, will there be buyouts, when will they happen, and what will they cost us from a cash perspective?

Modeling the changes in the OC Domain makes the process much less painful. Using the Business Activity Framework for each decision, we look at relative reductions in cash$_{OUT}$. We should also consider any cash investments involved in executing the act because they too, will affect cash$_{OUT}$. Doing so will create a complete picture of what is spent, when, and to what extent cash$_{OUT}$ reductions will occur.

All of these factors affect cash and must, therefore, be documented.

Specific Management Action

Once we understand the business changes and the management action necessary to achieve the benefits at a high level, we now have to create a more detailed plan of action. In the inventory example, if we understand that we need to increase the rate of output or consumption of inventory, the question is, what specific steps need to be taken? If through sales, how, specifically, will that happen? Will there be price discounts? Will models in inventory be upgraded with newer technologies to make them more appealing to potential buyers? If so, what technologies will need to be added, to what products will they be added, who is responsible, and when will that happen? Are there cash investments involved? If so, how much and when? What is the expected impact? If we are looking at other disposition strategies, what are they, when will they happen, and who is responsible? If, for instance, you want to give inventory away, how much will be given away, to whom, when, and what are the financial implications to cash$_{OUT}$ such as changes in tax rates or taxable income? As mentioned previously, there will be uncertainty associated with these actions, so bounding the opportunity might make the more sense than point projections.

Document Timing of Changes

We should now have a good idea of what changes can happen as a result of the improvement, who is responsible, and when management actions can or should happen. This step involves capturing and coordinating the information. Once captured, a story can be created about the project and the anticipated benefits. We know the overall cash value proposition from adding up all the value opportunities, how it is being enabled, what management steps are required, and when the changes will happen. We now take this information and plot it chronologically so that we can see what happens when, and the timing of the anticipated changes.

The information should also be used to consider the potential risks of the project. First, when considering the timing and dependencies of activities, do the steps make sense? Are the dependencies documented properly and in the right order? When considering risk, what are the implications if certain actions do not happen successfully? How does this affect the ability to realize the value proposition? These and similar questions help define high-risk critical areas that are imperative to identify and address to improve our cash value realization. Second, when considering resource commitments, does the work required align with the resources required and their availability? It is at this step that you ask tough questions about the implementation schedule, required resources, and the timing. This is when you move activities up or back to address resource consumption rates.

Project Cash Value Realization

This is the key information for creating cash-based benefit projections. We should know at this point the timing and rate at which spending will change, why it will change, risks, and what specific actions will be necessary to achieve the benefits. This should allow us to create an extensive projection of expenditures and cash value realization (Figure 8.7). We will discuss this more in Chapter 9.

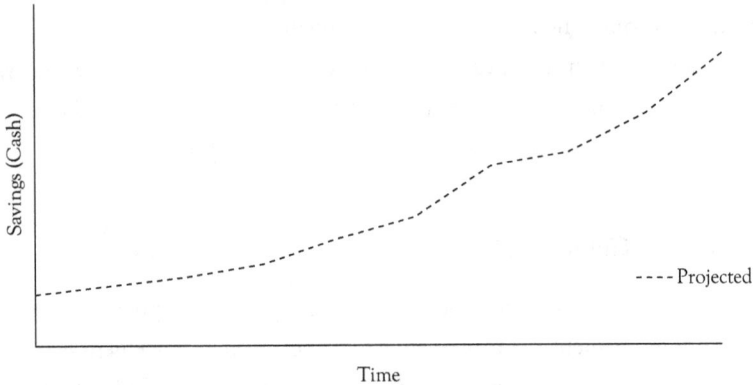

Figure 8.7 With all key information regarding the timing of management action and anticipated changes to cash$_{IN}$ and cash$_{OUT}$, we can project rate of cash value realization

Key Takeaways

1. When projecting the cash impact of the project, focus on cash$_{IN}$ and cash$_{OUT}$, and the factors that affect both. If something does not affect either, it will not impact cash. Use capacity maps as a guide.

2. It is important to be diligent about what steps need to be taken to realize the benefits. These steps may require investments of their own. We will want to minimize the impact of not achieving the value from missing key steps.

3. When projecting the benefits, it's best to bound the opportunity by creating an upper bound and a lower bound. Each boundary should have a list of assumptions tied to it that help leaders understand what is necessary to achieve that value.

CHAPTER 9

Benefit Realization, Accountability and Governance

To realize cash benefits, action must occur. With each action, there should be a plan that will document the steps needed for value realization. This will include the activities involved, the responsible individuals, comparing actual value realization to projected, and managing the inevitable variances that will exist.

As mentioned in Chapter 1, arguably, the most important step with improvement projects and realizing cash benefits is execution. Without execution, activities necessary to realize the benefits will not happen. With poor execution comes the potential for poor results. This chapter focuses on how to execute to ensure benefits will be realized to the greatest extent possible. The five steps that will help improve the quality of the execution and to help ensure that desired cash benefits are realized are:

1. Identifying the steps to value creation;
2. Identify responsible party or individual;
3. Determine cash value realization;
4. Assess and manage variances;
5. Capture positives and negatives for use with future project.

Identifying Steps to Value Realization

To this point in the book, we have discussed what is necessary to ensure cash value realization with our implementation projects. It starts with documenting, specifically, how the project increases the efficiency of capacity. As mentioned previously, there will be steps that must occur to realize the cash value by taking advantage of the efficiency improvement. With the improvements and requisite steps to improve business performance documented via capacity maps in the OC Domain, we look for the excess or residual capacity that may exists to identify ways to either reduce $cash_{OUT}$ or increase $cash_{IN}$.

These steps need to be included in the final project implementation plan and have to be acted on to realize improved cash value. One of the challenges I've made to those practicing lean, for instance, is that the programs do not go far enough in terms of realizing cash value. Most implementations stop at the business value step.[1] Lean focuses on the elimination of waste. This will increase the efficiency of the input capacity but unless specific steps are taken to change input capacity levels or what we pay for input capacity, companies are primarily just moving down the isocash curve, thereby realizing *cost* savings without necessarily achieving *cash* savings. What is necessary, instead, is to determine what improvements to capacity can be made as a result of the elimination of waste, and describe the steps necessary to realize the improvement. Lean typically does not go so far as to focus on reducing $cash_{OUT}$.

Say, for example, you want to get rid of excess slow moving and obsolete inventory for space purposes and to get the inventory off your books. There are several steps involved including, but not limited to activities such as identifying the criteria for inventory to be considered slow moving or obsolete, identifying the inventory that meet those criteria, identifying disposition options, modeling the financial implications of the disposition options, identifying demand for the inventory, agreeing on the transaction, agreeing on the timing and method of the inventory transfer, executing the transfer, organizing remaining inventory to take advantage of the extra space capacity created, and capturing the transaction in the company books. This would be an example of the steps involved in value realization from reducing slow moving and obsolete inventory.

---

[1] R.T. Yu-Lee. 2011. "Proper lean accounting." *Industrial Engineer* (October): pp. 39-43, R.T. Yu-Lee. March-April, 2006. "Determining the Financial Value of Implementing Lean." *Journal of Corporate Accounting and Finance*, pp. 79–88.

Identify Responsible Party

Once we've identified the steps in detail, we will need to identify the person who is responsible for executing the steps. Most ideal is when they are a part of the process of scoping the management action, but even when they are not, we want names to assign to actions as soon as possible. Too often, not only are the steps to achieve value not identified, when they are identified, there is initially no responsible person chosen to lead the effort. Many steps to handle inventory disposition, for example, should fall under the supply chain group while others may be tied to accounting and possibly sales. The individuals responsible for managing the disposition activities should be selected well before implementation. This is important for the following reasons:

1. When the project is being scoped this person can ask clarifying questions, challenge assumptions, and help set the direction and the action plan;
2. To assist defining governance;
3. The implementation team can get commitment from those responsible for the implementation.

Scoping

As steps to achieve changes are being identified, the person responsible should be actively involved in validating the steps and defining how the changes will be executed. They will be the person making the decisions, coordinating activities, and who understands the risks, so their input should be sought regularly here to execute the changes properly.

Governance

Resolving governance issues is critical when it comes to execution, and the responsible individual can help with governance strategy. One of three situations is often the case. The first is that the person responsible for making the decision does not have the authority to do so. They may find an inventory disposition partner, but does not have the authority to conduct a business transaction with them. The second scenario is when a decision needs to be made but no single person has been identified to own the action. For instance, an agreement is made for there to be a transfer of inventory, but no one with knowledge of how to make this happen has been assigned the task to do so. The third is when there is an overlap in governance, where multiple people or groups may be responsible for management action or execution. What if, for example, both merchandising and supply chain were responsible for managing inventory in a retail setting? These two groups may have opposing performance metrics, as merchandising may want to maximize gross margins while supply chain wants the inventory gone. If both are partially responsible for managing inventory levels, how are decisions made and executed? What may be good for one may be detrimental for the other.

There is a risk associated with inaction here. By not establishing governance, steps involved in value realization may meet with resistance or inaction, and that will create more risk, which puts cash value realization in jeopardy. With establishing ownership and discussing challenges associated with executing the plans, risk mitigation plans can be put in place. For example, if the organization realizes that, by reducing inventory via reducing prices to increase demand, certain merchandising metrics may be affected negatively, the organization may suspend the impact of the negative metrics for merchandising personnel for the overall good of the firm. This happened at a customer who was a large computer manufacturer and whose inventory turns policy became a constraint for a solution deployment group's ability to deliver solutions. This constrained revenue. After showing the operational, cash, and accounting impact of relaxing the requirement, we were able to increase the deployment rate by 150 percent, thereby increasing sales and cash$_{IN}$.

Commitment

The final step is the commitment to action by documenting ownership of the various steps. Once defined, we can create plans to execute the project and assess progress on the managerial steps. Figure 9.1 represents an example of a chart that has been used successfully to represent the steps necessary to achieve the value, the responsible individual, and the rate of execution. A chart like this can be used by project managers to assess the progress toward executing the necessary steps by the responsible individual.

Objective: Write-off obsolete and slow moving inventory (~$0.5M inventory value) Start date:														
Item	Action	Responsible	Due date	Complete (%)										Observations
				10	20	30	40	50	60	70	80	90	100	
1														
2														
3														
4														
5														
6														

Figure 9.1 This is an example of how we can document the management actions required, the person responsible, and their progress toward completion

To assess progress, for example, you can use percent complete and fill in the boxes with green, which means the activities are on task, yellow, which is caution suggesting there is a risk of missing deadlines, and red, which signifies a problem, so that attention and resources can be applied to the issue to ensure progress can continue in an effective way.

Determine Cash Value Realization

As the steps are being executed, progress toward realizing value is occurring. Teams should document when this happens, and the size of the value realized. As such, a cumulative tab for the amount spent and saved can be kept and reviewed, and the information can be represented as a curve representing cash value realization (Figure 9.2).

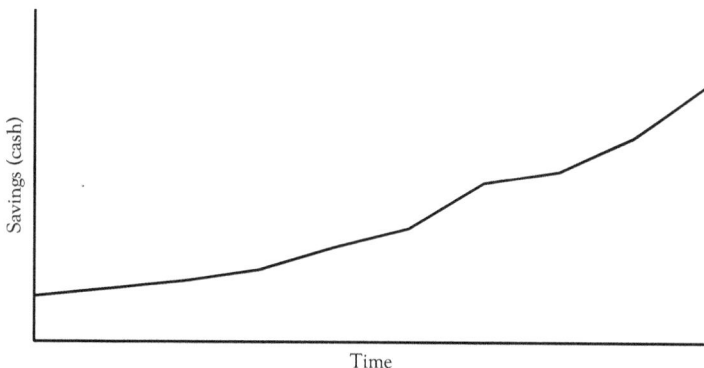

Figure 9.2 Through implementation, cash value will be realized. This value can be shown in a cumulative value realization chart

Manage Variances

In this step, we then compare the actual realization to the projected realization via reviews and audits (Figure 9.3). When comparing the two, we will likely come across variances, differences between what we expected to happen and what did happen. There are four key factors that lead to this variance:

1. The value opportunity is larger or smaller than expected;
2. Activities happened earlier or later than expected;
3. Value realizing activities did not occur at all;
4. Additional value realizing activities were identified and executed.

As you go through key milestones, it will be important to note the variances and the cause of the variances. If the variance is a timing issue, overall project value realization may remain the same, but the realization schedule may be accelerated or delayed. If the variance was caused by incorrect assumptions, these assumptions should be documented. This will allow the team to explore other options in the hopes of salvaging some of the initially defined cash value if the impact of the incorrect assumptions is negative. When positive, the assumptions can be shared in case they can improve performance on other projects. Either way, the expected cash value should be adjusted accordingly. It is important to note this

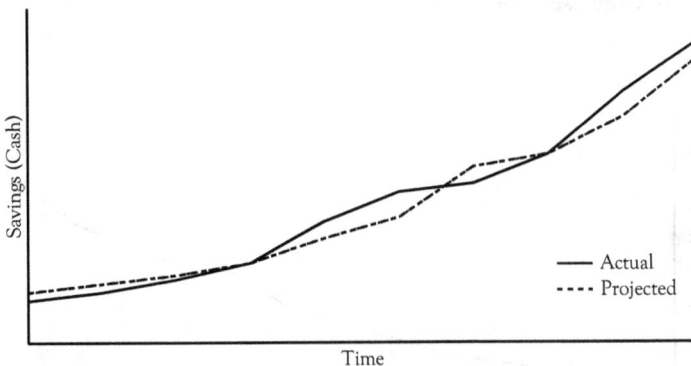

Figure 9.3 When we have our projected benefits, we can compare the projections to actual value realization. The variances can be discussed to understand the sources of why reality differs from the original projections

may affect other areas of the project, so those, too, should be updated as appropriate.

After discussing variances, there should be a set of activities identified to improve or document the variance.

Capture Positives and Negatives

Throughout the entire improvement project process, several assumptions have been made and many activities have occurred related to the project and project management activities. Some of these were good and should be incorporated in future projects or with project management activities. Some were not and should be excluded from future projects. These learnings should be documented and shared so that future projects can realize greater benefits in the future.

Key Takeaways

1. Execution is key, but it is beyond just execution. We should diligently plan our benefits and compare our realization rate to what was planned.
2. It is important to identify the owners of the managerial actions. This will ensure you have someone who owns the process when implementing and that you give them the ability to provide input to the activities they will be leading.
3. Governance is important. Ensure those responsible for implementing have the ability to act and that their ownership is clear.
4. Variance management is also important. Value opportunities can slide or, worse, disappear when not managed and the leaders are not held accountable for their realization.

Closing Remarks

This book is about cash value realization. Hopefully, I have added value to your understanding and approach to cash value realization. It is important to pay attention to certain details. For instance, if you want cash benefits, you must manage cash. This is where I believe most companies compromise their implementations. Too often, I hear leaders and consultants tell me they understand cash when, in fact, they still resort to accounting information such as costs and profit.

I wish you luck with your improvement projects, and I hope this book will help truly save you money when it comes to wide-eyed consultants and salespeople whose primary motivation isn't your success, it's theirs.

Cheers!

Reginald Tomas Lee, PhD, 2022

About the Author

Dr. Reginald Tomas Lee is a business analytics professor at Xavier University and a corporate advisor for Business Dynamics & Research, Ltd. He is also the author of *Strategic Cost Transformation, Lies, Damned Lies, and Cost Accounting, Essentials of Capacity Management*, and *Explicit Cost Dynamics*. He has also written and more than 40 articles and white papers. He has advised major brands, such as Toyota, Dell, Disney, The Home Depot, Bristol Myers Squibb, and DuPont. He and has worked for GM, IBM, Oracle, EY, and Miami University. Reginald has a PhD in mechanical engineering from the University of Dayton.

Index

OTHER TITLES IN THE PORTFOLIO AND PROJECT MANAGEMENT COLLECTION

Timothy J. Kloppenborg, Xavier University and
Kam Jugdev, Athabasca University, Editors

- *Lean Knowledge Management* by Forsgren Roger
- *Moving the Needle With Lean OKRs* by Bart den Haak
- *The MBA Distilled for Project & Program Professionals* by Clark Brad
- *Project Management for Banks* by Dan Bonner
- *Successfully Achieving Strategy Through Effective Portfolio Management* by Frank R. Parth
- *Be Agile Do Agile* by Vittal Anantatmula and Timothy J. Kloppenborg
- *Project-Led Strategic Management* by James Marion, John Lewis, and Tracey Richardson
- *Hybrid Project Management* by Mark Tolbert and Susan Parente
- *Design: A Business Case* by Brigitte Borja de Mozota and Steinar Valade-Amland
- *Workplace Jazz* by Gerald J. Leonard
- *Stakeholder-led Project Management, Second Edition* by Louise M. Worsley
- *A.G.I.L.E. Thinking Demystified* by Frank Forte

Concise and Applied Business Books

The Collection listed above is one of 30 business subject collections that Business Expert Press has grown to make BEP a premiere publisher of print and digital books. Our concise and applied books are for...

- Professionals and Practitioners
- Faculty who adopt our books for courses
- Librarians who know that BEP's Digital Libraries are a unique way to offer students ebooks to download, not restricted with any digital rights management
- Executive Training Course Leaders
- Business Seminar Organizers

Business Expert Press books are for anyone who needs to dig deeper on business ideas, goals, and solutions to everyday problems. Whether one print book, one ebook, or buying a digital library of 110 ebooks, we remain the affordable and smart way to be business smart. For more information, please visit www.businessexpertpress.com, or contact sales@businessexpertpress.com.